Lord Davi

Lord David Harris was born in the county of Kent in the South of England as Paul David Harris. After leaving school at the age of fifteen with no qualifications he was enrolled as an apprentice in a Naval Dockyard. After two years he decided he was not suited to the kind of work opportunities on offer and left to go into the entertainment industry.

He has worked as a performer, producer, director and broadcaster, as well as writing for radio, television, theatre and various magazines.

Since discovering his new lifestyle method and researching it for many years, he began to realize just how much it was changing his life. He now concentrates on holding seminars, life coaching sessions and motivational speaking.

He gained his title in 2017 when he became known as Lord David Harris.

THE SECRETS OF BRAIN POWER

YOU CAN HAVE IT ALL

INTRODUCTION

UNLOCK YOUR LIFE

What does 'Unlock Your life' mean? It means that we are all locked into our lives in many ways. We have our little routines and by and large stick with them for many years, most of our life in some cases. We all too often come to accept whatever life throws at us and more often than not assume that that is the best we can expect. Yes we might make the odd gesture, kick at the traces sometimes, but usually these are just tiny changes to our routine, going on a different kind of holiday, changing the car, re-decorating the living room. They don't really change much of the way we live our lives. Wouldn't it be great though if you could choose parts of your life that you are unhappy about and change them, or even change every single aspect of your life as you know it. In this book I will tell you how I changed everything about my life almost without realizing it was happening and show you how you can have anything and everything you have ever wanted. A better job, better relationships, more money, all can be achieved if you really want them and are determined enough to get them. You just have to use your brain.

Our brain controls everything about us, from how and when we breath to what we think and how we act, but most people's brains are not used to anywhere near their full capacity. We use them to suit ourselves, and our lifestyle as we see it. There are lots of things that the brain does automatically without any conscious input from us. Breathing for instance, making the various organs in the body do their jobs, kidneys, liver, heart and so on. All these and of course many other things the brain does for us. We don't have to think about them, in fact it would be rather strange if we had to think 'I'd better get my kidneys to filter my urine', thank goodness the brain does all this thinking for us.

Other things happen when we decide we want to do them, such as, learn to do our jobs, learn to read, cook, drive etc. we consciously make the decisions to do, and instruct our brains to take in and process the information as we collate it. That however is only a tiny part of the brain's function, the largest part of it we never use, rather like your computer, we mainly use what we need to get by in our careers and social life, the remainder of the functions that are available in the brain are locked away in the same way as are all the many things your computer can do that are never called upon to be used.

The brain is far more powerful than can ever be imagined, it has the power to easily change your life and give you anything your heart desires. I discovered the method that enables anyone to do this over a number of years and now I want to share it with you. This book explains how I came across the method and how you can use it to change every aspect of your life or just the parts that you feel need change. To do this you must learn to unlock the part of your brain that you have so far never used and learn how to use it to your advantage.

I had of course heard of ways to improve your chances of success in life and career and had even read books on the subject over the years, but although I thought them interesting my cynical brain didn't for a moment believe that much of what they propounded could work.

Many years later in a reflective moment I began to realize that certain important issues in my life had apparently been resolved without any conscious input from me. Sometimes without me even wanting the conclusions that had been reached but that nevertheless had turned out to be the correct ones.

I started to research the subject and as I got deeper into it gradually realized that certain events that had happened, seemingly automatically, during my life could be harnessed and used to solve similar problems that appear in everyone's life now and then and in this way help to gain more success in both career and life in general. The more research I did and subsequent changes I made in the way I lived my life seemed to make parts of my life fall into line as never before. The solution to a happier and much more fruitful and more successful life had been in front of me for many years but I just had not recognized it for what it was. It was as if my eyes had suddenly been opened to expose a form of living and thinking that had in effect been locked away for most of my existence. Throughout my life it seemed as if I had been shown tantalizing snippets of how life can work to bring success and anything else that one could want but was all locked away behind a door. Eventually I came to realize that if I were able to unlock that door everything I needed to know would be there and all I had to do was to learn to put that knowledge into practise and my life would then be enriched no end. This new way of living, or rather dealing with my life, had been right there, before my eyes, for years but only now had I seen and understood the clues, and been able to put them all together so I could start to use them on a daily basis in every part of my life.

I cannot begin to explain just how much my life has been changed since I metaphorically unlocked that door. The more I studied and practiced it the more I realized that it is all there in front of everyone, young or old, highly educated or barely educated, whatever your background all you have to do is recognize it for what it is and begin to use that knowledge. Unlock that door and you will unlock your life.

CHAPTER ONE

It's a funny old life isn't it? Why is it that some people can fall into a pit of sewage and come up smelling of roses, while others fall into a pit of roses and come up smelling of sewage? Some of us seem to swan through life doing everything right, good school grades, good marriage, great job. Followed by some lovely kids, job promotions, and eventually a good retirement with a very good pension. The rest of us stagger through life from low point to high point and back to low point and just hope that we find more high points than low as we meander through life's peaks and troughs towards a belt tightening retirement.

For many years my life was like the latter, good and bad, up and down. I can't in all honesty say I've had a terrible life so far. I've had some great times but along the way I've had my fair share of illness, both mental and physical, relationship and financial problems and a career that has had more ups and downs that a sex workers knickers. There were many times, particularly at the start of my career, when I have had to go without food and couldn't afford the rent on the small apartment with the damp patch on the ceiling and the mold on the bathroom wall. Times when I have been months without work and worried sick about where the next penny would come from. Bills were hidden away unopened until I had no choice but to borrow the money to pay them. Looking back, what is now obvious to me however is that none of those hard times need have happened. During my life I have been presented with several chances and ideas that could have greatly improved my life and career but at the time they were put in front of me I failed to recognize them for what they were, ignored them and carried on with my chaotic lifestyle. I will explain how these ideas and chances came to me and, more importantly, how they can help you, in much more detail, in future chapters.

Some people, much like me in the early days, can be given every chance in the book and either not realize what they've been given or think they know better and wander on through their life in their own sweet way. I knew of a family where the father was unemployed and along with his wife and two children were living in a rented Housing Association house on a run down estate rife with drug and drink problems. They were struggling along on benefits waiting for the next cheque to drop through the letter box so they could replenish the fridge and maybe have enough left to pay one of the many accumulated bills, when, out of the blue they won £100,000.00. I cannot now remember whether it was on the lottery, football pools or whatever, but this was in the 1970's when one hundred thousand pounds was a very great deal of money considering the average house in Britain cost around ten thousand pounds at this time. Just over one year later they had spent the lot and had nothing to show for it. They still lived in the same old rented house on the same estate, still drove an old clapped out car and the father was still unemployed. All the money had gone on parties, holidays, second hand flash cars and so on. With that kind of money they could have put down a sizable deposit on a house, or even brought one for cash in those days, brought a nice new family car, had a darn good holiday and still put a few thousand pounds by for a rainy day.

I am sure their friends and relatives gave advice on what to do with such a large sum but they chose to ignore any advice and go their own sweet way and ended up back where they started. Of course they probably had a great year but had they spent it wisely they could have had many great years. As I wrote a little earlier, some people can fall into a pit of roses and still end up smelling of sewage.

Despite my ups and downs over the years my life has gone from being one of mediocrity, bordering at times on disastrous, to being absolutely wonderful and if you carry on reading I will show you how you can turn your life into something better than you ever imagined and how to get most everything you ever wanted. I call this the 'BUSY' method for reasons that will become obvious as you read on. I discovered this just a few years ago even though certain parts of it had been put in front of me many years before and ignored or not understood. If you follow me on this trip of a lifetime you will learn how I turned my life around and learned to love the smell of roses.

If you accept and use even just a small part of the advice in this book it will help improve your life, but if you can follow all the advice, and stick with it, this could easily prove to be the best and most important book you will ever read. In the first part of the book I will explain how I eventually came across the BUSY method, how it worked for me, sometimes without even realizing it was working towards helping me learn how to use it. I will list the main components and explain why they work as they do. In the second part I will demonstrate how to put the various components together and how to make them work for you. I call this the BUSY method because those four little letters stand for what I know worked for me and can therefore work for anyone. BUSY stands for:

BELIVE IN YOURSELF. UNLOCK YOUR MIND. SUCCESS IS YOURS.

We are our own worst enemies. The human body is a wonderful thing and is capable of curing itself of many ailments, but many of us, unintentionally or more often than not, intentionally, do great harm to it during the course of our lives by putting the wrong fuel into it, not exercising enough and generally not keeping it in good condition. Food is fuel to our body. If you own a car that runs on a petrol engine and on a trip to the filling station you accidently put diesel fuel into the tank you will have made an expensive mistake that causes harm to the engine. It can be put right by the mechanic of course but at a cost. Likewise if you do nothing to keep the car in good condition it's bodywork, it's interior and it's engine will deteriorate.

With our bodies when we put the wrong fuel in, or even too much of the right fuel, it will cause harm, although more slowly than the wrong fuel in the car engine. Overtime though if we don't look after ourselves, we become, too fat, too thin, or contract various conditions, some of which will be life threatening. A great percentage of what happens to our bodies and what conditions or diseases we contract are a direct result of what we do to them. It is our fault. Yes of course we can always shift blame around, it's the advertisers, the newspapers, the television commercials telling us we deserve a few more cream cakes or a box of chocolates, but come on, we all know eating too much of the wrong food or drinking too much of anything is bad for us and causes our bodies to deteriorate.

It is not just the wrong food we eat that affects us, it's also the way we live our lives, lack of exercise, smoking, too much alcohol and stress all lead to the deterioration of our body. We pay for this just the way we have to pay for the car to be repaired after we've filled up with the wrong fuel and abused it. We pay with the aches and pains we get, the medicines we buy to alleviate the conditions that the wrong lifestyle has brought upon us and of course the years lost when our lives end.

The good news is that we can get back some of those years, get rid of the aches and pains and save some money by not having to buy the medicines. In theory it is very simple to do, eat better and less, stop smoking, drink less alcohol, exercise more. We all know what the answer is but most of us don't do anything about it, or we determine to do it and then fall at the first fence, and anyway life would be too boring if we didn't enjoy a few drinks or take-away meals now and then and spend a day or two laying on the couch catching up on a box set of your favourite television series. I was the same, I didn't exercise enough and I ate too much of the wrong food and my life was far too sedentary.

So what is it that causes us to behave like this and do these things that are obviously harming our bodies and perhaps even shortening our lives? Why can't we stick to a healthy living regime? Why can't we get that promotion at work that we think we deserve? Why can't we earn more money? And why do we so often fail when at last we determine to do something about it? The answer is easy, it is our brain, the organ that gives us our personality and controls everything we think and everything we do. It is the power source of the body. Without it we are just a lump of meat, bone nerves and sinews.

Can you imagine what an amazing organ this is? Not only does it control our physical actions and thoughts it also regulates our unconscious bodily processes, our breathing, digestion, and all the actions of our other organs, liver, kidneys and so on. Humans don't have the biggest brains, animals such as elephants and whales have brains much larger than us but we have the most developed brains of any living species. Proving that it's not the size that counts, it's what you do with it. Now where have I heard that before?

So given that we all have this wonderful organ nestling in our heads why can't we take control of our lives. Maybe lose weight, get a better job, earn more money and in general improve everything about our life. We know the brain controls everything we think and do as well as making us who we are, so why won't it improve our lives?

The simple answer is that we don't know how to use it properly. There are so many different ways of using this incredible part of our body that we haven't even dreamed about yet. Scientists discover new facts about the brain every day. They now know that the brain consists of around 100 billion nerve cells, known as neurons and it is these that form the power base that make the brain do what it does. Although our brain weighs just about 2% of our total bodyweight, it controls and manages 98% of everything we do, everything we think and how we behave.

Every human brain has the power to improve your life in any way you want. Relationships, finances, career and everything else that we can't begin to figure out how to get, our brain can help us to achieve if only we were to know how to use it more productively.

Now though, you can get all these things and much more, because I have discovered why things don't always work out as we would wish and how to change that to our advantage and get almost anything you have ever dreamed of.

This is not a magic solution to end all the problems that crop up during your life. This is a method that will help you learn to use your brain in a more productive way. To train it, if you like, to work better than it has been doing and to find the many more functions that it is capable of that most of us know nothing about.

To explain, think of your computer. Most of us own one these days but we only use the functions that we need to use to help with our everyday lives, both for personal use and in many cases for work. So, we might, for example, use emails, messaging, spread sheets, downloading music or videos and so on, but there are thousands of other things it can do that we don't use or even probably know about, things that could really enhance and make our lives easier and happier. We could go our whole lives not knowing about any of these programmes because we have got into a routine of using the computer in a way that suits our personal life and work. We stop looking for new methods and programmes because, 'this is the way we always do it.' Occasionally of course we might discover, or are told, about another function of the computer and we bring that into our daily routine but we still though ignore thousands of other functions and programmes that could make our lives easier and more productive. In other words we 'lock on' to what we need the computer to do for us and 'lock out' most of the other functions.

The same goes for your brain. We only use it in ways that suit our lives and possibly careers and we need to find a way of bringing into use more of the functions contained in the brain that we so far ignore or don't understand, thereby using what we have all been given to our best possible advantage. We need to open the door to the millions of other functions and programmes that the brain already has installed in it. If you put the BUSY method and tips I give in this book to full use you will start using more of your brain's functions and be able to improve your life no end. Whether you want to improve your career, your health, your finances or your relationships, this method, if used correctly, will enable you to achieve anything you want and get anything your heart desires, yes, you read that correctly, anything you desire. Your brain is locked on to the functions we need it for but locked out of the millions of other things it can do for us this book will show you how to unlock your brain and thereby:

UNLOCK YOUR LIFE.

CHAPTER TWO

We all make mistakes in our lives but the biggest mistake of all is to try to change things too quickly. We've all done it. A month before you go on holiday you decide that you must lose 15 pounds before you can be seen on the beach and decide to go on a strict diet. You want to see results in a week or so and when the results are just a tiny drop in your weight, you lose heart and give up after a few more days of half-heartedly trying. If you are lucky and very determined you might lose that amount of weight but a couple of weeks after the holiday you put it all back on plus a bit more.

Here's another scenario that is all too common. You decide to give up smoking and after a couple of weeks of gasping for a cigarette but resolving never to give in, something comes along to upset you, or you're at a party with friends, you've had a couple of drinks and you are offered a cigarette. You think to yourself that one won't hurt, and what happens, you light up. The following day you decide to have just one more then within two or three days you are back in the old routine.

Preparation and determination are the secrets of success. I smoked two packs of cigarettes a day for many years and tried many times to give up the habit. Sometimes this would last a few days before I gave in to my cravings, one memorable time I gave up for just over a month before I went back to the habit. Each time I would decide that I would definitely give up this time and would stop smoking immediately, throwing the remaining cigarettes into the bin. Or I would tell myself I am definitely giving up from tomorrow. This was my big mistake and I made the same mistake every time, my will-power would be strong for a few hours then gradually get weaker and weaker until I gave in to my cravings. After many attempts and just as many failures, I woke up one Christmas morning with that familiar dry mouth, bad breath and usual craving for that first cigarette and I wasn't even out of bed yet. For some reason, unknown to me at the time, the thought came into my head that I would give up smoking on my birthday. My birthday, by the way, is six months after Christmas on June 25th. I had six months to think about it and as the weeks and months went by I found myself becoming more and more keen for that date to come round so that I could give up. "Only three months more". I would tell myself. "Only six weeks more," and so on. By the time it got to May I was still smoking forty cigarettes a day but wanted to pack up there and then. However I knew that I had to carry on until my birthday in late June. By the time my birthday came along I couldn't wait to give up, it was the most natural feeling as if I had finished a job and was happy to walk away from it. From that day to this I have not smoked another cigarette and to my surprise there was no craving and the desire to accept a cigarette when offered disappeared from that day on. It has been over twenty-five years since I last smoked and after suffering and failing many times before I couldn't quite believe that this time it could be so easy. Thinking about it many years later I realized what must have happened, once I had planted the fact in my brain that I really wanted to give up but couldn't think of a sure way of doing it my brain took the problem over and had been subconsciously working on it until it had found the solution and popped it into my head that Christmas morning, a perfect Christmas present. Had I rushed into it once again and given up my smoking habit that day I'm sure I would have failed like all the other times.

So the brain can sort a problem without you realizing it is already working on a solution. This invariably happens when we are asleep, during what is known as REM (rapid eye movement) sleep, when we are usually dreaming. Scientists from the PSL Research University in Paris, France, have discovered that the brain can also learn during this REM sleep. They played white noise to volunteers whilst they were asleep and found that only the noises played to them during the REM sleep could be remembered when they woke up and the noises played during deep sleep were forgotten. So the brain can solve certain problems during REM sleep. You have to start the ball rolling but then just leave it to do its job. I had been determined to give up smoking and my brain had prepared the way.

Determination and preparation.

There are other components needed, apart from determination and preparation, to be able to use this BUSY method successfully and at will, which I will explain in future chapters. Essentially it is down to the individual to learn and take control of the method thereby making much more use of your brain and unlocking more of the amazing power contained within it.

You may be thinking is this just yet another self-help book, sometimes also known as self-improvement, of which many have been published over the years and many readers of them, who have attempted to follow the advice within, have failed to make any significant improvement in their life. So perhaps I should take time to explain exactly what a self-help book is, why they sometimes don't change people's lives and why some people have become skeptical of the whole genre.

Firstly any non-fiction work can be classified as a self-help book. Think of the instruction book that comes with your new car or household appliance, its purpose is to help you learn about the product, how to use it and look after it. It improves your knowledge of the product so in that sense could be classed as a self-help book. Likewise a book about another country helps improve your knowledge of that country, a biography helps improve your knowledge of the subject, so again, most, if not all non-fiction works are in one way or another self-help or self-improvement.

Possibly the first self-help book specifically aimed at helping improve an aspect of people's lives was published by a man who dedicated his life to helping people improve their lot. Dale Carnegie was an American who started his career by holding classes in public speaking. He found that many people had a great desire to become more self-confident and his classes went on to help many achieve this. He started the courses in 1912 and his first book, 'Public Speaking', was published in 1926. His greatest writing achievement was undoubtedly, 'How to Win Friends and Influence People', published in 1936. By the time of his death in 1955 this book had sold five million copies and has continued selling ever since.

Despite selling in there millions why do many avid readers of various books in this genre fail to make any significant changes in their lives? In the past I have read maybe two or three of this type of book all of which promised I could change my life completely and what is more could have anything I wanted. I would usually put into practise what the author recommended I do, to make all my dreams come true, then, after a couple of weeks, without winning the jackpot on the Lottery, my cynical brain would start explaining to me why this couldn't possibly work. If the advice in this book could really guarantee me anything I wanted, I would reason, then why is the author bothering to sit down for many months to hammer out this book, instead of just getting everything he wants and spending the rest of his life sitting on a sun soaked beach somewhere in the Caribbean, sipping champagne. It didn't occur to me that one of his wishes could have been to write a best selling book or maybe he just wanted to share his good fortune.

The truth is though that most readers of these books give up following the advice after a few days or at most a few weeks, as indeed I did. Although it has to be said that even if we had persevered for years the chances of winning a lottery jackpot with odds of around 1 in 457million against are pretty slim, would you back a horse at these odds and expect to win? Most people would wish for something and expect it to fall into their hands within a couple of days as if by magic but this is not the way most self-improvement methods work. It is a process that has to be learnt in perhaps the same way that you had to learn to use your computer. You start by reading the instruction book and probably make mistakes along the way but if you persevere you eventually become proficient. So, just like learning your computer, for some people it will be fairly easy to master the method while others will find it much more difficult and therefore take longer to learn the basics, but ultimately everyone has the inbred ability to succeed.

So as I have explained that most non-fiction books are in many ways self-help or if you like, self-improvement, I prefer to call this an instruction manual. Follow the instructions and you really can change your life or the parts of it that you feel need changing. It is not a series of weird semi-magic unproved theories dreamed up by me. All the things I suggest I have used myself and seen them completely change my life. They have all been researched and tested many times, sometimes over years, by research centres, scientists and universities throughout the world.

I stumbled on this amazing, life changing, method almost by accident and I can assure you it has helped me change my life immeasurably. The advice I give in this book cannot only bring you a much happier life in general but can also improve your health, your finances, your relationship with your partner, or even help find you a partner if you don't already have one.

It can even help you find a new career and change your life completely if that is what you are looking for. How can I be sure that this book and the advice in it will bring you these wonderful changes to your life? The truthful answer is, I can't guarantee that everyone who reads this book will suddenly become wealthy and find the love of their lives because I cannot guarantee that you will follow the advice properly. What I can say is that if it has worked for me it can work for anybody. After all, as I stated earlier, I was a cynic and a pessimist but not anymore, what has happened to me in the autumn of my life would be unimaginable to the young me. All you have to do is follow the advice and see the changes it can make for yourself.

And by the way, if you are already saying to yourself, 'If this works why is he writing a book instead of sitting on a Caribbean beach sipping champagne'. I can tell you after five minutes of sitting on any beach I would be bored silly, and I don't like champagne, but I do love writing. I have written for radio, television and the theatre, as well as magazine articles and books, so I hope that answers your cynical thoughts and you stick with me and learn the secrets of the BUSY method and use them to improve your life and to have more confidence in what your brain can do for you. BUSY will also help make you into a happier person with a much brighter outlook on life.

How nice it would be to wake up in the morning feeling happy and optimistic about the day ahead instead of waking with a gray cloud of apprehension hovering above the bed. Of course bad or annoying things happen to everybody from time to time and these can't always be avoided but with the BUSY method you will learn to look at these as minor blips in your day rather than viewing them as yet another disaster designed to ruin your life.

CHAPTER THREE

To explain how this life-changing method came to me I should start by telling you about my early life and how my eyes re gradually opened to these amazing possibilities for improving it. Even though at first I didn't realize what it meant or what could be done with this knowledge that was drip-feeding into my mind.

My life, like most peoples I suppose, was a bit like a roller coaster, there were months or sometimes years when everything seemed to be an uphill struggle. Other times everything seemed to be going along swimmingly and I was enjoying my life as a young adult. At first I was in the wrong job but didn't know how to get out of it or what I wanted to do. Then when I finally managed to get into the career I wanted, I chose possibly the most insecure career there is. I went into the entertainment business. There would be periods when work was scarce and I couldn't pay the bills, followed by good periods and then just as I was getting back on a even keel along would come another lean period to knock me back again, but then as they say 'That's showbusiness'. I got mainly short term contracts, sometimes a few weeks, other times maybe a few months work and an awful lot of one day jobs. I managed to pay the rent and eat, although I did have to go without meals occasionally in the early days, when I had run out of money and there was no work on the horizon. In general though I managed but never seemed to be able to take that next step. I couldn't move from effluence to affluence. As the song says "Good times, bad times, I've had them all'. And after many years of this kind of life I gradually realized the answers were there right in front me, but even then, knowing what the way to a better more fruitful life was, I still did nothing about it. Why?

The reason I decided to do nothing about it was because of something called conditioning. When I was in my teens and early twenties I was told on many occasions that I was no good and would not succeed at anything. My teachers at school would leave me to my own devises at the back of the class because, as they told me on more than one occasion, I was a dunce, the class clown, so for most of my time at school I just kept my head down and was ignored by the teachers. At home my father rarely spoke to me, apart from shouting at me now and then. I certainly can never remember having a conversation with him. I genuinely don't remember him ever talking to me apart from the odd few words, usually telling me off about something or other. It was just a case of "Do this" or "Don't do that", and that was about the extent of my relationship with him. My mother, who was basically a good mother but obviously had little faith in me, would never encourage me in whatever I wanted to do. I remember when I told her I was going to leave home and get my own apartment, she said that I could never manage on my own and would be back begging to come home again within three months. When I told her I was going to stop smoking she told me I would never do that because I didn't have the strength of mind to do it. When I told her I was leaving my job and going into the entertainment business she told me that I would get nowhere in that business and if I was determined to do that not to expect any help from her. So from when I was around thirteen until I left home at the age of twenty-three, when I finally got my own apartment, I got no encouragement for anything.

Now, years later, I know that this conditioned me to think I was no good at many things and would not succeed. I had my dreams of course, of having a good life, a good career, earning lots of money and so on but subconsciously I knew I couldn't because my mother, father and teachers had told me so many times that I would get nowhere. If you are told something often enough, after a while you begin to believe it.

I should point out here that I firmly believe a parent can condition their child too much the other way with equally bad results. If you tell a child often enough during their formative years that they are brilliant at everything and can do no wrong they can then grow up believing this and therefore do not try to get on with their life because they don't think they need to work at it. They just blame everyone else when things go wrong. So, like many things, a balance is needed in everything, a young person needs encouragement but also reining in occasionally, so that eventually they end up as a well balanced person.

When I was fifteen I was told I was to leave school without any qualifications. I wasn't consulted of course it was a stitch up between my mother and the headmaster. She had made up her mind I should become an apprentice in Chatham's Naval Dockyard, as that was the main employer in the area where we lived and not having given any thought to a career because I assumed I would be at school for another two or three years, I went along with it. I took the entrance exam, and a few weeks later found myself as an apprentice shipwright in Her Majesty's Dockyard, a job I was totally unsuited for and had no interest in. It was eighteen months of hating every minute of it and realizing that I would never make a half decent shipwright, and had I stayed on and finished my apprenticeship our Navy could have been in dire trouble. That was when I began to think about what I really wanted to do for a career and how I could get out of my five year naval apprenticeship. I decided that a career in the entertainment business would suit me. I have no idea why I thought that, I'd had no training and didn't even go the theatre apart from perhaps seeing the Christmas pantomime as a young child with my family. I knew nobody in the business and hadn't the slightest idea how to get into it. All I knew was that the idea had popped into my head from nowhere and I made the decision and that is what I was going to do.

After a few months of thinking about a career in entertainment, things just started to happen, as if out of my control. I remember standing at a bus stop when the bus came along and stopped right in front of me I noticed a small advertisement, in the bus window, for a pantomime at a theatre in Tunbridge Wells, a town on the Kent/Sussex border, a town I had never visited, which was some fifty miles from where I lived. The advertisement stated 'Alan Gale presents Little Red Riding Hood at the Opera House Theatre'. I know now that this was well out of date as it was March and the show would have closed in January. At the time I didn't realize that, but somehow the bus company hadn't got round to taking the poster down and as I looked at it I just knew that I must write to this man named on the poster, who I imagined, in my ignorance, was still presenting Little Red Riding Hood, at the Opera House Theatre in Tunbridge Wells.

I wrote him a letter to the theatre, thinking he must still be there, or perhaps even lived at the theatre. He of course was long gone but some kind person forwarded the letter to his home address and after a few weeks I got a reply in which he said it was far to early to be casting for next years show and as I had no training or experience in the theatre, there was nothing he could do for me. I had all but forgotten about this episode but still had this feeling in my mind that I would be working in the entertainment world, when, in some three or four months later word went round the Dockyard that some shipwrights were being sent to Devonport Dockyard in Plymouth. In conversation with fellow workers I declared that were I to be asked I would refuse to go because I knew nothing about Plymouth, which was 250 miles from home, and didn't fancy going there to continue my apprenticeship anyway. That same evening when I got home from another dreary day in the Dockyard, there was a letter waiting for me from a man saying my letter, that I had written to Alan Gale several months before, had been passed on to him and asking me if I would be interested in auditioning for a show he was producing. Intrigued and excited I phoned the number at the top of the letter and agreed to go to London for an audition. It didn't occur to me that I had no idea what an audition was or what would be required of me but I just knew I had to go. We arranged for me to go to meet the man on the following Sunday, November 5th at his home in South London. Without telling anybody I caught the train to London and found my way to the address in Blackheath an affluent area of south London. I don't even remember feeling nervous about the meeting I just assumed it was the right thing to do. Luckily I wasn't asked to audition, it was more of an interview and after about half an hour of him asking me about my experience, none, and my ambitions, many, he offered me the job, at a theatre in Plymouth, the very town I could have ended up in had I stayed in the dockyard, and this turned out to be the start of a long career in the entertainment business.

I was just eighteen years old and at the time I didn't think about how this had all happened, I assumed it was just luck. However many years later after an very much up and down career in the business I began to think about how I got my start and realized that luck, on its own, doesn't exist. Questions kept forcing their way into my mind. Why was the original, out of date, poster on the bus not taken down? Why did Alan Gale pass on my letter to another producer many months after I had written it? After all there are thousands of students coming out of drama schools and universities every year looking for a start in the business. Why did the producer take me on even though I had no experience or as far as he could ascertain from a short interview, talent?

What happened, I decided, was that if you plant a seed in your mind and keep nurturing and turning it over it will eventually grow and find the solution you need. Most of the hard work is done subconsciously by mind power. I am sure many of my readers will have at times gone to bed thinking about some problem or other that they can't find a solution to, only to wake up in the morning when the answer to the problem just pops into your mind. Your brain has worked on the problem during the night, while you were fast asleep and found the answer for you.

Another great example of how my brain found a solution to what I thought was an unsolvable problem, was how I came to buy my first house. I had been living in a rented flat for many years, which consisted of the two lower floors of a very large, four story, Victorian house. It looked rather like something from a horror movie set, although it was in one of the best parts of town. Ten wide cracked steps, green with age, led up to big double front doors that creaked loudly when opened. You entered a large hallway with a long uncarpeted staircase edged by a heavy polished mahogany banister leading to the upper two floors that were rented to an elderly, rather strange, couple who I found out later had been there for many years. The rooms were typical for the period with very high ceilings and large windows in every room each one with original wooden shutters which when closed were fastened by heavy iron bars.

One day a friend, who had just brought his own house, asked why I hadn't thought about buying mine. I gave him three reasons, 1: I was unemployed, 2: I had no money at all and was living on benefits, and 3: As far as I knew the place wasn't for sale. I dismissed his suggestion out of hand, there was no way anyone would give me a mortgage even if the place was for sale, and if it had been I would surely have known. The next morning when I awoke the thought popped into my head that I should at least call the landlord to find out if he was thinking of selling, because if he was I would have to start looking for somewhere else to live.

I called him and asked if he was thinking of selling and he said that he hadn't thought of it but that any of his properties were for sale at any time although none of them were on the market at that time. When I asked him to give me an idea of what sort of price he would be willing to sell my place for, I thought the figure he mentioned was rather high for what amounted to half a house, but while talking further it transpired that the price he would be asking was for the whole house, in other words both flats.

I knew there was no way I could afford it even if I managed to find someone to lend me the money. My friend, however, persuaded me to call the banks and building societies to ask. Of course they all turned me down because the building had a sitting tenant in the upper flat and anyway I didn't have a few thousand pounds for the deposit, so that was the end of my home owning dream, except it wasn't. A few days later a leaflet came through the door advertising a building society seeking clients to save with them. I had never heard of them but something told me I should call them and ask about getting a mortgage, I don't really know why I was bothering because there was no way I could raise a deposit, even if I had been working. To my surprise they said they would lend me ninety percent of the purchase price if I could meet their conditions, the main ones being that I could afford the repayments and had the remaining ten percent deposit, neither of which I could of course. The thought of owning my own house kept swirling around in my brain even though I knew there was no chance of finding the deposit and convincing the building society that I could afford the repayments on unemployment benefit.

Then a week or so later a friend, who ran a theatrical agency, called to offer me a job, only for one night, to entertain in a hotel. I did various jobs for him but they only amounted to around ten or so nights each year, but I accepted this job that was in a weeks time. He also said that I could possibly work in the hotel on a permanent basis as an entertainment host if I wanted. The same day a letter arrived from the building society asking for details of my employment, they were obviously pursuing my call to them thinking it was a serious enquiry. Just for fun, or so I thought, I replied to them stating that I worked for the friend who had just offered me one nights work and multiplied the money he was paying me for the night by five days and then fifty two weeks coming up with an annual figure. Which is what I thought the salary would be if I took up his offer of a permanent job. After I had sent the letter I started to panic and called my friend, the agent, to tell him what I had done. He said he would confirm my figure if they contacted him so that I wouldn't look a complete fool. It didn't worry me that it was probably fraudulent because there was no way I could go through with it without the deposit. A few weeks went past and I got another letter arranging for their surveyor to call to put a value on the property. I should have told them I had changed my mind but out of interest I thought it would be good to find what the value was in case at some time in the future my situation changed and I could think of buying. The surveyor came and valued the house at ten percent more than the price the landlord was asking, this meant that the amount the building society were willing to lend was the complete asking price, so I was now able to buy the house without having a deposit. I'm certain no one could buy a house in this way these days as the rules have tightened considerably but a couple of months later I was buying my flat and the one upstairs and it had all happened almost without me realizing what I was doing. Around this time work started to come in on a more regular basis, although the permanent job at the hotel didn't come to fruition, I was still able to make the monthly payments without too many problems. So I had no money, was unemployed at the time yet somehow my brain had worked out a way for me to get what I wanted.

This wasn't the end of the saga though. I had been living in the house quite happily for a number of years when a further example of mind power, involving the house, was about to happen to me. I had invested in a theatrical costume and scenic hire business with a partner that went disastrously wrong. I was at this time still in the entertainment business doing quite well, managing to pay the bills and still had the sitting tenants upstairs. Then came the day that I was informed that the business I had invested had all gone wrong. I was a silent partner and knew nothing of the day-to-day workings of the business, the partner who ran it had kept me in the dark about the problems and the upshot was that the business collapsed and he walked away. Shortly after I was informed that the bank was owed £53,000.00 and as the ex-partner had no assets I was held to be responsible for finding this vast amount of money. The only assets I had were the two flats but I obviously didn't want to end up homeless and the tenants in the other had been in there since 1939 and it was now the late 1980's and there was no sign of them moving out. They had informed me many times that they were there until they died. They were also on a controlled rent, which meant that a council officer decided what rent I could charge, which was never very much, and I could only apply for an increase every three years. So with a small rental income, I had not made any profit from the flat, the rent they paid didn't even cover half the mortgage on the house.

In the meantime I was getting letters and calls from the bank wanting to know how I was to pay this vast debt, the interest on which was mounting up on a daily basis. There was nothing I could do except to put my flat on the market , hope there would be enough equity in it to pay the bank and make myself homeless. If I had tried to sell the other flat with a sitting tenant which I was sure at the time, would have been very difficult if not impossible, it wouldn't have raised enough to pay off the bank, so I had no choice but to sell my home. I registered with an estate agent and started thinking about where I could find somewhere to move to when my flat was sold. I don't think I have ever been so worried in my life. A buyer was found after a couple of months and the solicitors started doing all the necessary business. Contracts were exchanged, completion was to be four weeks later and I still had nowhere to live or even to store all my belongings. On the day that we exchanged contracts I got a phone call from the son-in-law of the upstairs tenants informing me that his mother and father-in-law were moving out of their flat at the weekend. They were not good tenants and didn't get on with me, so we seldom spoke. They had been in the flat for nearly fifty years with no intention of ever moving out but, without knowing anything about my situation, they moved out giving me just three days notice and a place to live. My flat sale went through giving me a healthy profit after paying off the bank and I still owned the other flat. The building society agreed to secure their mortgage on the upper flat, which I then moved into and lived there happily for several more years. Eventually I sold it for ten times what I had paid for it some years before and brought a very nice house in a nearby village.

As you can imagine this whole terrible business had been going round and round in my mind with what I thought was no way out except to make myself homeless but once again my brain had sorted it all out for me.

I had for the second time stumbled on a method of getting what I wanted. I wasn't sitting around thinking 'poor me, isn't life unfair'. I was worried sick of course but was also determined to find a solution and subconsciously my brain had worked it out for me. I never did find out why my tenants had decided to move after nearly fifty years in the house. They never told me they were going, apart from the call from the son-in-law, and on the day they moved they just put their keys through my letterbox without even saying goodbye. After I had settled into my new apartment I began to realize that I now knew the secret to getting whatever I wanted, but to make it work better, to refine it, I knew I had to find out why this works and how to make it work for me always and not just when I had problems. I was still working, on and off, in the entertainment industry, mainly in theatre productions and cabaret but started to spend more of my time trying to figure why this had worked without seemingly any conscious input from me. I also needed to establish if there was anyway that I could learn to take control of this power and use it whenever, and however, I wanted. Eventually after a lot more research and work I came across the other components that helped make it work just as and when I wanted.

CHAPTER FOUR

So many people from all walks of life tell me they are unhappy with the way their life is going. Unhappy or frustrated for all sorts of reasons, maybe their career is in a rut or their relationship has gone stale. It could be because of financial problems or sometimes they feel everything about the life they are living is not the life they expected or indeed wanted. There are many annoying things that can unexpectedly come along to de-rail a seemingly good life. A redundancy that then exposes flaws in a relationship when the breadwinner becomes a stay-at-home partner and money becomes tight. Health problems can put great pressure on what seemed to be a reasonable life style, bad housing, bad neighbours or a relationship that has just gone stale can all turn a pleasant enough life into an unhappy one.

There are though lots of people living unfulfilled, or unsatisfactory lives who do nothing to try to remedy this because they just assume that it is meant to be. That's the way life is and there's nothing to be done about it. It is how they have come to expect their life to be and they must just accept their lot. However there is no reason to live a life that makes you unhappy, bored or lonely. Do not accept the bad things in your life, there is always something that will remedy any situation.

Let me try to explain why so many people have and accept what they might describe as disappointing lives, struggling from one pay day to the next, working in a job they don't enjoy and generally leading a pretty boring life.

Years ago I had a very good friend and neighbour, a married lady with one child. Her husband was self-employed and worked hard at his job. Over the years, my friend took various menial jobs to help out with the family budget. She worked as an office cleaner, supermarket shelf filler, and similar low paid positions. She hated the jobs but said she needed to work to help bring in a little more money. They lived in a nice little terraced house that they managed over the years to buy but that was all they had of value. In all the years I knew them they never managed to have a family holiday, their vehicle, which the husband needed for his business, was just a succession of elderly vans and they had almost no social life. They seemed happy enough but always struggled to pay the bills on time and never managed to have any money left at the end of the month to save for their future. They were just working to live and in the twenty five years I knew them their life never changed. No matter how hard they worked they could not get out of the rut they had started out in. Sure as the years went by they spent on the house, new furniture, carpets etc. but always brought on credit and carefully budgeted for, they certainly didn't waste money. They were working class people living a working class life. So why, despite working hard and not wasting money on gambling, booze or expensive hobbies and never being able to afford family holidays, could they not get out of that rut?

The reason, I am convinced, is that deep inside they didn't think they deserved to. This was their place in life and they had to accept it. During many conversations with them over the years if I mentioned about somebody going on an exotic holiday or buying a new expensive car or house, they would always say, "Very nice, but that's not for the likes of us", or "People like us don't have those chances". They put themselves down all the time and convinced themselves that their life could never change for the better and of course it never did. If you convince yourself that you are not worthy of a better life then of course you won't get it.

People convince themselves that they can't do things. How many times do you hear people say, "I'm hopeless at D.I.Y." or 'I can't cook", and if they then try they make a mess of it because they have convinced themselves they are no good at it. Think about it, we are all born the same, nobody is born with the ability to cook or decorate the living room, they are all skills that have to be learnt and anybody could learn them. The usual reason we don't bother to learn certain skills is because we are not interested in them, which is fair enough, but we are all interested in having a better life so why not learn to have one. You only have to read the problem pages in newspapers and magazines to see the sort of sad lives some people are living. Bad marriages, poor housing, dead end jobs. When faced with problems like these is it any wonder that people give up hope and spend their lives just plodding along year after year with just the occasional bright spot. When with the help of the BUSY method they could brighten their whole life, career, relationship, financial, every aspect of anybody's life can be made infinitely better.

YOU CAN CHANGE YOUR LIFE

Anyone of any age or education can change their life, it doesn't matter if you want to change just one thing or everything about your existence, the only thing that can stop you is you. You must stop making excuses for why you can't or shouldn't do it. I'm too old, too tired, too stupid. Nobody is completely inept in this world. I had a friend who couldn't read, couldn't write and was useless at any kind of figures but he was a brilliant gardener and automatically knew what to plant where and how best to make it thrive. He was also amazing with animals and an excellent horseman. He had some kind of what could possibly be described as a psychic connection with all animals and birds. Working for a council parks and gardens department, looking after the plants trees and gardens, he was considered the best and most knowledgeable man on the team. One day he was walking home from work and he came across a duck walking along a busy road, fearful that the bird might get run over he told it to follow him and it did, it followed him all the way home and lived in his garden for many months. The duck seemed settled and never tried to escape although it had free run of the garden and could have left at anytime. It followed my friend everywhere and would do anything he asked of it. Some people thought him stupid or ignorant because he couldn't read or write but he was much cleverer than most with animals and gardening. When he was in his mid-thirties he decided to change direction and start his own business, which he ran successfully until retirement. Everyone has the ability to change their life no matter what the odds against it are. Just read the following stories about some of the people who have done just that against, what must have seemed to some to be insurmountable odds and you should be convinced that even you can follow the BUSY method to enhance a part or all of your life, the choice is yours.

In the twenty first century many civilized countries throughout the world operate some kind of benefit system and pensions. So although it might be considered by some to be too little, it is there to help citizens when they are in ill health, disabled, unemployed or of pensionable age. However these are a comparatively recent addition to the modern way of life. If we go back a few hundred years there would be very little, if any, kind of help for people in need, who were poor, sick or dispossessed, but even in those hard times certain people still managed to turn their lives around despite seemingly insurmountable problems. Here are a few examples of some of those people.

IF THEY CAN DO IT SO CAN YOU

Matthias Buchinger was born in 1674 in a town near Nuremberg in Germany. He was born without legs, feet and arms, having just two deformed, flipper like, hands attached to his shoulders. He was also of very short stature never growing to more than 29 inches tall. With no financial help available he had the choice of becoming a beggar or finding a way to earn a living. He chose the latter and taught himself painting and drawing, holding brushes and pencils in his mouth, magic tricks, dancing and calligraphy. He also played six different musical instruments and became a recognized marksman with a pistol, demonstrating many different kinds of trick shots. He spent his working life selling his drawings and paintings as well as entertaining the public with his conjuring, dancing and shooting. Many times he performed several shows each day, at Holburn, a small town near Southampton, he advertised performances at 10 o'clock, 12.00, 2.00, 4.00, 6.00 and 8 o'clock. He worked hard at promoting himself and his shows and despite his many disabilities eventually became world famous and managed to earn a good living right up until his death in around 1740. Although working hard from the age of twelve until his death at the then great age of sixty six he still managed to marry four times and father fourteen children.

Physicist Albert Einstein is rightly considered to be a genius. He has won the Nobel prize and changed the face of physics with his Theory of Relativity, but his journey to worldwide fame was not an easy one and he was certainly not considered to be the right material to become the genius he would later prove himself to be. Born in 1879 in Germany, he didn't learn to speak until he was three years old and was unable to read until he was seven. Known as a reluctant student he was expelled from one school and refused entry to another, finally dropping out of school altogether at the age of fifteen. During his schooldays his teachers and his parents thought perhaps he could be mentally handicapped and would only be suited to a menial job. He left Germany to avoid conscription into the armed services and eventually managed to enroll at the Zurich Polytechnic but on graduation his professors gave him a pretty bad recommendation owing to his skipping classes too often and his rebellious nature. He ignored all the negative comments certain in his own mind that he would get to the top of his chosen profession and eventually, as we know, he became the genius that the world knows him to be. Even being offered to become president of Israel, an offer he declined, but not a bad career for a boy who couldn't read until seven who was expelled from school.

American Oprah Winfrey is best known for her award winning talk show that became the highest rated programme ever on any channel on American television. However if anyone was born to fail one could be forgiven for thinking it would be Oprah. Born in 1954 in Mississippi, her teenage mother was unmarried and revealed that Oprah's conception was the result of a single sexual encounter. Shortly after giving birth her mother moved away leaving her new born baby with her grandmother. They lived in abject poverty with Oprah often being dressed in clothes made from potato sacks and being bullied by the local children because of this. She was raped at the age of nine and over the next few years was regularly abused and molested by her uncle, a cousin and a friend of the family, she finally ran away from home at the age of just thirteen. A year later she prematurely gave birth to a son who died after a few days.

Despite this shocking childhood Oprah went to school and gained a scholarship to Tennessee State University where she studied communication. From her first job as a teenager in a local grocery store she was offered a job on a local black radio station, which became the launch pad to her career in radio and television. She is now considered by many to be the greatest black philanthropist, ever, in America, having given away over $400 million to educational causes. From her poverty stricken start in life she has fought her way to become possibly the most famous, admired and wealthiest African American woman in history.

Joanne Rowling, better known as J. K. Rowling, has been named, by magazine editors, as the most influential woman in Britain. Sales of her books have netted to date £230, million. She went from being penniless and on state benefits to being a millionaire in just five years.

Born in Gloucestershire, England, her initial school days were unexceptional and she has stated that her teenage years were unhappy, mainly because of her difficult relationship with her father, who she doesn't see or speak to anymore. She was turned down for Oxford University but eventually accepted for the University of Exeter where she recalls doing not very much work. Her first marriage lasted just about one year during which she suffered a miscarriage but gave birth to her daughter in 1993.

She saw herself as a complete failure being a single mother and jobless while trying to bring up a child. Eventually being diagnosed with clinical depression and even contemplating suicide, she applied for benefits and described herself as being "as poor as it's possible to be in modern Britain, without being homeless".

J. K. wrote most of her first book in what was to become the Harry Potter series, 'Harry Potter and the Philosopher's Stone', partly in a local café because she couldn't afford to heat her home. After finishing the book it was turned down by no less than twelve publishers before one decided to take a chance and publish it. She has since become the best selling children's author in the world and is also considered to be one of the wealthiest. One of her sayings, that is often quoted, should be taken to heart by everyone with a wish to improve their lives. It is yet more proof that successful people who have beaten great odds to get to the top of the ladder, know that the secret to becoming successful is within ourselves already. This is what she said:

"We do not need magic to transform our world. We carry all the power we need inside ourselves already".

There can't be many people in the world who have not heard of 'Kentucky Fried Chicken', or KFC as its known today. Colonel Sanders, the inventor of the recipe and the brand was born in Indiana in the south of America in 1890. Harland Sanders, his real name, was just five years old when his father died and his mother had to leave home to find work leaving Harland at home to look after his siblings and even cook all the family meals. When his mother remarried some years later Harland had, what has been described as a tumultuous relationship with his step father, so at ten years old he went to work as a farmhand and finally left home for good at thirteen.

Over the next forty years he took many jobs including, a blacksmiths helper, cleaning the ash pans of trains and various laboring and sales jobs. He then studied law through a correspondence course, a career move that ended after a courtroom fight with his own client.

While working at a Shell Service Station in the 1930's he started selling fried chicken from his home, next to the service station, to raise some much needed cash, however the business failed when World War Two broke out, just after he had finalized his 'secret recipe' for fried chicken. He suffered several more failed businesses over the following ten years and it wasn't until 1952 when he was 62 years old that he franchised his secret recipe calling it ' Kentucky Fried Chicken'. The business expanded rapidly and by 1964 had more than six hundred outlets, when the Colonel decided to sell the business as he was by now 73 years old. His eventual success is further proof that age has little to do with the process, Colonel Sanders was 62 before he changed his life and fortunes, so, no matter what age you are success can still be yours.

There are, of course many thousands of people all over the world who manage to change their lives to various degrees despite enormous difficulties and often seemingly insurmountable odds against them achieving their dreams. The Paralympic Games are a perfect example of ordinary men and women determined to win against all odds. The games involve hundreds of athletes from many different countries and cultures with a range of disabilities competing in many different sports to the highest standards. The games are held in parallel with the Olympic Games and are usually held immediately after them both in summer and winter. Win or lose the athletes involved have all overcome their individual disabilities to prove that they can beat the odds and succeed in their chosen sports.

Are you still telling yourself you are unable to change your life after reading these stories? The people I have written about succeeded without the help of my BUSY method but learning and putting it into practise will show you how to change the way your brain works so that it will help you to get anything you have ever dreamed about.

All these stories above concerning people who have beaten tremendous physical and emotional problems to succeed in what they believed in, are possibly eclipsed by the man who's story I relate below. Although his problems were not so much physical, the emotional setbacks he endured during his life show just how high one can climb up the ladder of life while overcoming more problems than most of us would have to deal with throughout our whole lives.

The story involves an American family, their young son and the myriad problems that beset the boy throughout his life while trying to find a career that would enable him to support his wife and children. From a very young age he fought his way through everything that life threw at him with never a thought of giving up on his ambitions until he reached the very top of his career path. For him though there was not to be a happy ending, fate decided to deal him one more blow.

In 1811 the family, their, nine year old daughter and seven year old son, were thrown out of their farmstead home after a land dispute and the son had to start working to help support the family.

At 9 his mother died and he had to work even harder to support his sister and father.

At 16 his ambition was to go to law school, but because he was working all hours
he had had very little education and was rejected by the school authorities.

At 22 he was working as a store clerk but was sacked after a few months when
the business dropped off.

At 23 he ran for the state legislature but lost the vote.

At 24 he went into business but it quickly failed and left him with a very large debt that took him many years to repay.

At 27 he, unsurprisingly, had a nervous breakdown.

At 29 he tried again for the state legislature and once again lost the vote.

At 31 he was defeated in his attempt to become an elector.

At 35 he had been defeated twice while running for Congress.

At 36 he finally managed to be voted in.

At 39 he lost his re-election bid.

At 41 his, four year old son died. He had three other children only one of which grew to maturity.

At 42 he was rejected as a prospective land officer.

At 45 he decided to run for Senate and lost.

At 47 he was rejected for the vice presidential nomination.

At 49 he ran once again for Senate and once again lost the vote.

At 51 he was elected the President of the United States of America.

At 56 He was assassinated.

The man was Abraham Lincoln 16th president of the United States from 1861 to 1865. He is considered by scholars and many of the public to be one of the greatest of the United States Presidents. One of his quotes that we should bear in mind is:

That some achieve great success is proof to all that others can achieve it as well.

These are just a few stories of people who changed their lives regardless of the knocks they took along the way. For every one of these famous people who changed their lives there are thousands of other unknown men and women throughout the world who have also taken control of their lives and made up their minds to improve them. You can overcome anything with determination and self-belief

CHAPTER FIVE

All the people mentioned in the previous chapter succeeded through sheer will power, determination and hard work. You will have the benefit of my BUSY method, which will make it easier for you to get to where you want to be in life.

There are several components that go to make up my amazing BUSY method and together they can work miracles on an individual's brain. Some are obvious others not so but by putting them all together and getting in the right frame of mind all the components will work together to get you where you want to be and, don't forget, get you anything your heart desires. It is important that you learn and understand about all parts of the method and how to use them to your best advantage to change the way you live your life from day to day.

I am often asked many questions about how and why this method works so well and you will find most of the answers within these pages, however the three most frequently asked questions I think deserve more detailed answers to help you get the results you are seeking. So here they are:

HOW DO YOU KNOW I CAN CHANGE MY LIFE? ISN'T LIFE PRE-DESTINED?

Life is not predestined we all have free will and can make decisions for ourselves. If all life was predestined what would be the point of going to work or making any decisions about anything, we could just sit back and let it all happen.

You could leave the house today and get hit by a car, but although possibly not your fault it was your decision to leave the house instead of staying safely at home. When we are born we may inherit some of our parents looks and genes but apart from genetic illness, or debilitating conditions, that could be inherited from one or both of our parents, it is what is inside our head that determines how we become as we grow, and how we use our brain that determines our future. Obviously we are influenced by what we are told, what we see and the experiences we have, whether good or bad, as we grow up. Our parents, teachers and family members will advise and teach us all manner of things as we are growing, but how much of that knowledge is put to use is entirely down to us. Some people are more easily influenced by other peoples behavior, especially when young, but it is still up to the individual to decide whether to be influenced or not.

We have all come across young adults who have lead pretty fruitless lives, indulging in petty crime, in and out of dead end jobs, leaving a trail of unpaid bills behind them, all this despite having a good upbringing by hard working and honest parents. The opposite is also true as well, there are many very successful, hardworking people who come from dysfunctional or feckless families.

Young people, and to a lessor extent some adults, sometimes get in with the wrong crowd and end up getting into trouble and for some this defines their whole life and they go on to lead a troubled lifestyle. Others while still mixing with the same type of crowd eventually choose a different route and lead a reasonably blameless life. This is because some of us use our brains differently to others. Some people use them to define what the result of certain actions may be and then choose the appropriate path to navigate. Others live for the day without a single thought for what the consequences might be of their actions. In other words although we all have basically the same brain and are all influenced by other people, what we see, hear or read, ultimately we are all free to make our own decisions. Nothing is planned in advance for us, we are all masters of our own destiny. Everything relies on how we choose to use the power that we all have within our brains. Our destiny is in our own hands, or rather in our own heads.

We all make thousands of decisions every day of our lives, many of them made by our brain without us realizing. The brain makes these decisions for us, it tells us to breathe, yawn, cough etc. and arranges for our various organs to operate as they should, all are made without us having to think about them, others are what could be called considered decisions, we think about something and decide which action to take. We have several tasks to do at work or at home and we decide in which order to them, or we want a new job and have to decide which companies to send our resume to. Some people find it difficult to make a decision through laziness or fear of making the wrong one and therefore end up making none at all just letting their life drift by, not knowing where they are going or where they want to end up. This is the perfect recipe for an unfulfilling, unsatisfactory lifestyle, an unnecessary waste of what could be a successful and happy life.

In previous pages we have seen how people have changed their lives completely despite having a terrible start or encountering massive problems and knock-backs along the way, problems that would have defeated many others. They almost certainly made many wrong decisions along the way but understood that a wrong decision can teach them valuable lessons, like, what not to do if a certain situation appears again. So, rather than give up they learnt from those wrong decisions, refused to accept failure, carried on and eventually got to where they wanted to be.

I started out as a very shy adolescent, a failure at school who finished education at just fifteen years of age without any qualifications. I passed what was then called the eleven plus exam and from the age of eleven until passing my driving test, at the third attempt, at the age of twenty seven, I failed every exam I entered. I then drifted into a job that I was entirely unsuited for, where I managed to last for less than half of a five year apprenticeship before giving up on that. I then decided to go into a profession that I knew nothing about, had no training for and no idea how to get into, but somehow against all the odds I managed to get in and hang on to it for many years. I bumbled along enjoying some periods of reasonable success and many more periods of struggle. I constantly put the blame for the lean times, when offers of work were not forthcoming, on bad luck, the weather, the government and even on some mystical power that didn't want me to succeed. I had no confidence in myself or my abilities, although I was pretty good at disguising the fact and even if some of the failures in my career and personal life were clearly my fault I became a master at either ignoring them or placing the blame elsewhere.

Eventually, after many years, it slowly dawned on me that everything good or bad that happened in my life and career was entirely in my own hands and therefore if the bad parts were my fault, for not turning them into something positive, and the good parts were my doing then I should be able to take more control. I realized that I had to concentrate on the positive thoughts and learn to ignore the negative thoughts. Instead of waking in the morning thinking about things that might go wrong today, I had to learn to think about what will go right today and how good the day will be. I had stumbled on parts of the method that I would come to call the BUSY method, but it would still take some years before I discovered the other components of the method. Eventually I decided that if I put all the significant parts together and put them into practice I would have total control of my life. All I had to do was to search for and find the other components.

Slowly my life began to change, things began to happen and I wasn't quite sure how some of them had happened. From having too much month left at the end of my money I suddenly had money left at the end of the month but didn't seem to be doing any more work than I had before. I was happier and more optimistic about things in general and I acquired things, like a new car for instance, without having to pay on credit. I threw away my credit card, which had been my lifeline for many years and have never used one since. I now have a nice detached, four bedroom house for which I paid cash, I have significant savings for the first time in my life and no debt at all. I am happier than I have ever been and it seems as if my life has suddenly gone from being slightly out of focus to being bright, sunny and sharply focused.

If I can do this, believe me, anyone can. It is not necessarily easy, as you have to stick with it and convince yourself that it will work but if you do this you will improve your life beyond anything you ever imagined. You will become a happier more content and grateful individual and look forward to the future. In later chapters I will set out the ingredients and the method that will make this work.

HOW LONG WILL IT TAKE TO CHANGE MY LIFE?

I am often asked this question and it is the most difficult one to answer. It's like asking how long does it take to learn to drive a car or how long is a piece of string.

As with everything it is up to you how quickly you master my BUSY method and start to see the changes in your life. It will also rely on how many changes you want or need to make and how dedicated you are to making it happen. You will need to change the way you think and train your brain to work in different ways. This will naturally take more time for some people than others. The more focused you are the sooner you will start to see the benefits.

I have found that most people say that the hardest part is getting started. People read the book and think they will start it when they get time to concentrate on the method but, rather like I did in the beginning, they prevaricate and put off starting and if they are not careful their initial enthusiasm wears off and it becomes easier to find reasons why they can't start and the longer they put off starting the more difficult it becomes. So give yourself a date when you want to start and stick to it.

Some participants have dedicated themselves to the method and work hard and fast to achieve the results they are looking for, while others prefer to take a much steadier path and take their time. I wrote in an earlier chapter that in the early days I could see what I should do but ignored the signs, then eventually decided to study in depth, find the individual components and put them together rather like doing a jigsaw puzzle until the full picture began to emerge. Of course now I wish I had started much earlier and my life would have become the amazing life I am living now but years earlier. I am a typical Cancerian, born at the end of June, a crab, and just like the crab I take ages thinking about what I should do and summing up the possible benefits and drawbacks, looking at the problem from all angles and spending hours thinking about whether I should go ahead or not, but when I finally decide to go for it, just like the crab, I grab hold and refuse to let go under any circumstances. So if you just follow the instructions in part two of this book at your own pace, the results will follow when needed.

HOW DETERMINED MUST I BE TO GET THE RESULTS I WANT?

Determination is everything. You cannot go into this potential life-changing programme half-heartedly. Remember it is all in the mind, so if you follow the procedures laid down in this book, while thinking, 'I'll give it a try but I can't see how it can work'. Then it quite possibly won't work. The idea is that you must convince your mind that it will work, you must believe in the system and banish negative thoughts. If you are determined it will work, your mind will come to accept the fact very quickly and will work with you to help you reach your ultimate goal.

Of course you will still have days when you feel down, depressed maybe and think that life isn't fair and you are not getting where you want to be. Everybody has bad days when everything seems to go wrong. This is the time when it's easy to give up and just accept life as it comes and stop trying to improve things. Do not on any account give in to these feelings, instead use them to strengthen your resolve and make yourself even more determined. To help banish these negative feelings try to concentrate on some good positive feelings, something nice a friend said to you, a happy occasion, something you saw or read about that made you laugh. You can even listen to your favourite song, music is very powerful and can enhance your feelings or change them completely. Anyone of any age has the power in their brain to change their lives if they learn how to harness it and use it correctly. It doesn't matter if you are a teenager or a pensioner, unemployed or working, everyone has the ability and probably the need to improve their lives in some ways. Stop making excuses for yourself and certainly don't blame 'bad luck' when things don't go as you want them to. I think it was Richard Branson who, when somebody said they thought he had been very lucky, replied that throughout his life he had found that:

The harder you work the luckier you get.

Many people have the tendency to set their limits far too low on their ambitions. You might, for instance be a taxi driver working for a company and your ambition is to, one day, own your own taxi so that all the profits become your own instead of having to give a share to the company. Or you work on the factory floor and have ambition to one day, and with hard work, become the factory foreman. Now I realize that many people in this position would say they are quite happy driving a taxi cab or working in a factory, but ask them if they would be just as happy to do that job for five days per week for maybe forty eight weeks per year for possibly forty years and I'll wager the answer then would be in the negative, because most people don't think of their future that far ahead. Thinking short term is limiting yourself and why would you want to do that. Reach for the very top of the ladder, believe that you can get there and you will.

People say, "I know my limitations", but believe me most people have no idea of their limitations, they underestimate them and convince themselves they have limitations that don't really exist. Ask them if they could you run a marathon if they had no legs, or become an artist and paint beautiful pictures if they had no hands or arms, and the chances are they would say no, of course not, but these things have been done on many occasions by many people, so the genuine answer is yes you can. It is not necessarily easy but if you are determined then you can do it. So once again we come back to the fact that determination is everything. When a problem occurs in your life don't automatically go for the easiest solution to the problem, be determined to go for the best one, that way you solve the problem but also enhance your life at the same time.

Ray Kroc is a perfect example of determination in action. He was born in Illinois, America in 1902 and from the age of ten did odd jobs in order to earn his own money. During the First World War he lied about his age to become a Red Cross ambulance driver from the age of fifteen. After the war he worked in various jobs including a pianist and a disc jokey on a local radio station before going into sales for around seventeen years, selling paper cups and milkshakes. He even worked, for no wages, just his board and keep, in a restaurant to learn the business. During his time selling milkshakes he became involved with the McDonald brothers who owned a few small restaurants in San Bernardino, California. He offered to work for them for no fixed salary, just a small cut of the profits, and managed to save enough money in six years to buy out the brothers share of the business, becoming sole owner of the few restaurants the brothers had built up with his help. Determined to expand the business he automated and standardised the production of hamburgers and eventually franchised the business while only choosing new owners for their determination and drive. Within a few years McDonalds became the leading brand of fast food restaurants in the world and by the time of Kroc's death in 1984 McDonalds had 7,500 outlets in 31 countries and his personal wealth was estimated at eight billion dollars. Not bad for a milkshake salesman. Once he was asked for the secret of his success, this was his reply:

"Nothing in the world can take the place of persistence.
Talent won't; nothing is more common than unsuccessful men with talent.
Genius won't; unrewarded genius is almost a proverb.
Education won't; the world is full of educated derelicts.
Persistence and determination alone are omnipotent".

I'm sure you'll agree that this is a very wise observation from a man who proved throughout his life that determination was the main factor in allowing him to achieve the success that he had set his mind on.

Henry Van Dyke, was another man who knew the value of determination. He was one of the most influential, and well respected, men in the late nineteenth and early twentieth centuries. He was an American from Pennsylvania, born in 1852. He became a professor of English Literature at Princeton University, Minister to the Netherlands and Luxembourg and was elected to the American Academy of Arts and Letters. He was an author, poet, educator, and clergyman. Generally thought of as one of the wisest men of his generation, one of his quotes, made in the mid 1800's, remains very relevant today and particularly so in the context of this book. He said:

Some succeed because they are destined to, but most succeed because they are determined to.

CHAPTER SIX

CHANGE YOUR MIND

The mind, or rather the brain is a very complicated organ, it is the power source and computer that controls everything about our body. Even our most celebrated scientists don't yet fully understand it. However one thing they do know is that it can work for you or against you, sometimes without you even realizing it. If you tell yourself, or are told by others, often enough, that you will fail at a certain task, it is almost certain that you will. You will have convinced yourself or been convinced by others that you will fail and so you invariably do. Unless that is you do something to change your way of thinking. Most people are pessimistic in some ways, while some people are pessimistic in most ways. Even confirmed optimists can be seen to be pessimistic now and then. Pessimists always see the glass as being half empty, optimists see it as half full, but even optimists become negative at some point in their lives. People who are upbeat and optimistic most of the time will quite happily admit they can't do this or that or are useless at certain tasks and by telling yourself this often enough the brain will process this fact because it has been programmed to accept the fact. Whereas if you tell yourself repeatedly that you can do this task the brain will eventually, with practise, help you master these skills and you will become proficient at the very tasks you thought you were no good at.

A good example of how the brain can be fed and accept a fact that isn't true, process it and act on it, is the following incident that happened to a lady friend of mine. She was at home turning up the hem of some curtains and like many seamstresses do she was holding the dressmakers pins between her teeth. As she finished putting the last pin in she suddenly thought that she should have had another pin in her mouth. There wasn't one and the thought entered her head that maybe she had swallowed one. Obviously this worried her because if she had it could turn out to be rather dangerous to swallow a pin. The thought went round and round in her head and after half an hour or so she felt a pricking sensation in her chest. The feeling escalated over the next few hours until she was in quite a lot of pain and decided that she'd have to go to the hospital. In the accident and emergency department she told her story and was sent to the Xray department for an Xray of her chest, which revealed that she had not swallowed any pin and the cause of the pain was unknown. Within minutes of the xray proving that she hadn't in fact swallowed a pin the pain miraculously disappeared never to return. A perfect example of the brain being told something and acting on it even though there was no need for it to do so.

So, if the brain can act on a negative thought, like the one just described imagine this happening the other way round. You tell yourself something positive and the brain acts on that fact and starts working on the result that it knows the fact should have. You can tell yourself you will succeed at this and your brain helps you to succeed. You can imagine yourself getting promotion at work and your brain will eventually tell you how you should go about getting that promotion. Once your brain is unlocked to work in this way you can get anything you want. This is an extension of something called, the Placebo effect.

A placebo is a treatment or a substance that has no active therapeutic effect. Sometimes known as a sugar pill. It's a treatment that contains nothing that will affect the patient's health, except it does, and has been proved by scientists and doctors to work. In other words it is a fake treatment but it works for just the one reason that the patient's brain believes it will.

Placebos are used mainly in research to determine the effects of new drugs. One patient will be given the new drug that is being tested while another will be given a placebo, a sugar pill, though neither patient will know which pill they have been given. Scientists have discovered that sometimes the patient will have a response to the placebo. This could be an improvement in their symptoms or some other effect. Often the effects of the placebo seem to defy logic. In one study for instance people were given a placebo and were told it was a stimulant. A short while after taking, what was of course a fake pill, the patient's pulse rate and blood pressure increased and their reaction speeds improved. A few days later the same people were given the same pill and this time told it would help them get a better quality of sleep. It was then noticed that their pulse rate and blood pressure and reaction speeds decreased. In other words the patient believed a fact that wasn't true and their brain acted on it as if it was true.

Dr Jeremy Howick is a clinical epidemiologist at the University of Oxford who has spent several years studying research into the effects placebo treatments have. He reviewed 152 trials involving 15,000 patients with various illnesses or conditions, the results of which showed that placebos have almost the same effect as more traditional 'real' treatments.

There have been studies that show placebos can have an effect on some conditions even though the patient is fully aware that they have been given a placebo. Conditions such as depression, sleep disorders and even the menopause. These are just three of several conditions that seem to improve regardless of the fact that the patients know they are being treated with something that in theory shouldn't have any effect. It would seem that in these cases the brain starts to act because it knows that the patient wants it to, despite the patient knowing they have been given a placebo it appears to act as a catalyst, which seems to accelerate a chemical reaction within the brain. If you believe that something will help you then it almost certainly will. On the other hand if you believe something will make you ill then it probably will.

So now we know that the brain can have a positive or detrimental effect on your health, according to what you believe, and more importantly what the brain thinks you want. So can the brain have similar effects on the way you live your life? I believe, and have proved to myself, over the years that it can, it is just a question of belief both in yourself and in the changes you want to make. I will not only show you how to activate your brain to work in a more positive way but also how to look at your life in a totally different way. A way that can help start your brain working to improve every aspect of your life and enable you to get anything you want from your life.

If you believe in yourself, or in some cases believe in what you are told, the brain will take over and deliver the results that it thinks are required. Recently researchers, from the university of Bonn, in Germany, investigated to see if the placebo effect worked on different types of wine. They gave volunteers three samples of the same wine but were told that one was cheap, one was middle priced and the third was a very expensive wine. The volunteers were asked to give the three samples marks out of ten on the taste. The results showed that the more expensive they thought the wine was the better it tasted. The researchers used an MRI scanner to see what was going on in the participant's brain, as they tasted the wine, and decided that the placebo effect seemed to alter the brain's perception of taste. Another good example of the placebo effect is hypnotism. A patient who has been hypnotized is relaxed, has focused attention and increased suggestibility, meaning that they are more prone to believe what they are told. Irving Kirsch, Associate Director of Placebo Studies at Harvard Medical School, describes hypnosis as a "non-deceptive placebo". There have been many cases of medical procedures being carried out under hypnosis, even full invasive operations performed where the patient is awake throughout the procedure but feels no pain purely because he believes he will feel no pain, so his brain doesn't activate it's pain receptors. Therefore if you can persuade the brain that the patient will feel no pain whilst being operated on, it surely follows that the brain can be made to act in any way we want it to.

It is thought that the placebo effect works more often than at first we thought it would. Surgeons are now warning that some operations could be unnecessary because it is the placebo effect that benefits the patient rather than the operation they have just been put through. Studies have shown that keyhole knee surgery, arthritis operations and inserting gastric band balloons, used to help obese patients loose weight, all work mainly because people expect them to.

Neuroscientist Professor Irene Tracey, speaking at a recent Cheltenham Science Festival said that people wrongly dismiss placebos as deception and fakery. Studies are now going on to determine what, if any, results from certain operations are purely because of the placebo effect rather than the operation itself.

Throughout the centuries and even today in many countries around the world certain cultures and religions believe in the absolute power of witch doctors and faith healers. In southern Africa these people are known as Sangomas or Shamans and are held in high regard by the local populace. They are consulted on many issues and problems, which they believe the Shaman will have the power to solve. If, for instance, a member of the community has a health issue they will consult the local Shaman who will attempt to cure them of the problem. More often than not the cure will work perfectly well even though it might well have consisted of just a charm or some chanting from the Shaman. This, we would assume is one more example of the placebo effect. However Shamans are often consulted about many non-medical issues, grievances, relationship problems, revenge issues etc. The power of the Shaman is such that he might well decree that the guilty person who caused the problem will pay with his life within a certain amount of time and sure enough the person concerned does die, even though there is no medical reason that would cause their death. They believe they will die, so they do. They believe in the total power of the Shaman and the 'magic' he can summon to kill or cure at will. Whereas in reality of course it is the power of suggestion and not a 'magic' power available to the Shaman that causes the results he decrees.

This is yet even more proof of the enormous power held within the brain, a power that we should never underestimate. It is the most powerful machine, computer, intellectual bunch of neurons, call it what you will, that have ever been or ever will be invented and everybody in the world has got one for free. All you have to do is learn to use it to its fullest advantage. Most of us don't bother, we use it for what we need instead of using it for what we want.

A piece of 'equipment' as sophisticated, and amazing as the human brain hasn't evolved over millions of years without having the ability to deliver much more than most people expect of it. The problem is that most of us are sceptical by nature, 'If it sounds too good to be true, it probably is'. We've all heard that saying time and time again but this is true, the human brain can deliver anything anybody wants. All you have to do is believe.

Belief in yourself and the power within your brain is the secret to making my BUSY method work for you. The problem as stated in the previous paragraph is that many people are skeptical and tend to believe their negative thoughts. In fact it seems to almost be an inbred trait that a great percentage of the human race is generally pessimistic, if not all the time then some of it. However it doesn't matter how pessimistic you are or for how long you have been a pessimist, you can change and become an optimist and I can show you how.

The biggest mistake people make is, not believing they are capable of doing it. There have been many books written about improving lifestyles and thousands of people over the years have proved without a shadow of a doubt that it has worked for them. On the other hand many more readers of these books have tried implementing the advice contained in the books to no avail because they either give up early, when they don't see immediate results, or they ignore or don't believe results that do start to happen because they doubt their ability to make them happen.

Don't view your life as something that you have to put up with. Instead view it as a challenge you have been given and that you know you can win. It is entirely up to you whether you choose to win the heat, the semi-final or go for gold. Whatever route you choose it can take you to the winning post. You have the power in your head, all you have to do is learn to use it.

THE LADDERS OF LIFE

To enable you to do this it help's if you look at your life as a series of ladders that must be climbed one step at a time. There may be many ladders in your life but the main four in everybody's life are, the health ladder, the career or work ladder, the personal ladder and the financial ladder.

From the time we are born we automatically start climbing one of the ladders. A newborn baby is at the bottom of their personal ladder but very soon and without realizing, they metaphorically start to climb one step at a time. They will learn to sit up then crawl, then walk, so you see they are already three steps up their ladder. This continues throughout life a rung at a time until they get to where they are happy or content to be, and at that point they stop climbing.

Some people never stop climbing until they get to the top because they are ambitious and want to get the best out of life. Maybe they want to get to the top of their career or want to achieve great financial security, or even just want to keep in the best of health. If that's the case they might want to keep working at finding different ways of staying fit and healthy. Perhaps they want the best in their relationships, always trying to make them happier and more fruitful, working towards a better home life for them and their family, or maybe it's searching for the very best for their children, their education and their future. Whatever it is these people never accept anything other than the top rung of all their ladders.

Then there are other people who stop bothering to climb far too early and either assume that they are incapable of getting any higher or are content with where they are, even though they know there are many more steps they could climb. Of course there are always others who think they are up the top of the ladder even though they are not. With the help of my BUSY method, if acted upon with determination and by following my instructions, anyone can be sure of climbing further up any, or all of these imaginary, ladders. This doesn't mean anyone who attempts this will get to the very top simply because everyone's expectations will vary. Some will want to be on the top rung of the ladder they are climbing, whereas others will be happy rising just a few rungs and being content with where they are and feel no need to go any higher to enjoy a happy and fulfilling life. Others may decide they need to climb, for example, the career ladder but are quite content with where they are on the personal or relationship ladder.

Many people are too accepting of whatever life throws at them and assume they have no choice in the way life treats them. "It's all in the lap of the Gods," they say, but believe me it certainly isn't in anybody's lap. You have complete control of your life once you start to re-programme your brain. Use my BUSY method and you can change as much or as little of your life as you choose.

To clarify this issue of seeing life as a series of ladders, I want to explain more about why and how I see life like this. You have no doubt heard the saying, "I can't see the wood for the trees", in other words you can't see the situation clearly because you are too involved in it. That's why sometimes it is easier for another person to help when you have a problem because they can see only the problem whereas you see the whole picture with your particular problem hidden somewhere in it. So separating your life into a series of different parts, financial, career, personal etc. will immediately make them more visible and easier to deal with. This also means you can work on each part one at a time and when you are satisfied with where you have got to with one part you can move on to the next. You can, of course, work on all the parts at the same time if that's the way you like to work it just means you need to be better at juggling.

Let us take a closer look at the career ladder for instance. I am always surprised when I ask people what job or area would they really like to work in if they could do any job in the world, no matter how fanciful. Racing driver, film star, Prime Minster, ballet dancer, if any job in the world were available to you what would you choose? So many people answer "I don't know". Which is why so many people spend all their working lives doing a job they don't care for. If you have just finished your education and are not sure which career path you want to follow, that is understandable. If a person then goes into a certain job and after a while finds that it is not suitable and leaves, that is also understandable. However to go into a job that you realize you don't like but stay in it for years that is unforgivable and unnecessary. There are reasons given as to why someone would stay in a job they hate, usually because they have a family to look after, but there are always ways around this situation. If for instance you work in a supermarket filling shelves day after day and you really want to be a hairdresser then think about going to night school to learn the skill. So many people who have absolutely no idea which kind of job they would like, spend most of their time drifting through life doing something they don't want to.

Could you imagine starting a car journey with no idea where you want to go? It would be a complete waste of time. Obviously you would never get there because you won't know where 'there' is. You would be driving round and round, turning this way and that, wasting fuel, not knowing which direction to go in and when you eventually finish the journey, probably because you run out of fuel, you still won't know whether you want to be there.

It is the same with your working life, if you don't know which area you want to work in, or what type of job you want to do, you'll almost certainly end up working in a job you don't like or have no aptitude for. You'd be dreading the start of each new week and just waiting for the next pay cheque. Obviously not everyone could become Prime Minster but you could perhaps work in that area, a politician, an assistant, a secretary, even a cleaner in the Houses of Parliament. Even a lowly job like that means you are on the bottom rung but on the right ladder in the right area, now if there is a chance to take a step up you are at least in the right area to take it. This is an extreme example but you can see what I mean, decide what you want to do and get any job in the right area so that if a chance to move up the ladder comes along you are ready to make a grab for it.

Or supposing you want to be a racing driver, the top rung is probably a world class Formula One Champion, the bottom rung is learning about the industry and exploring job opportunities. Now of course very few of us would reach the top of that ladder but again, with hard work and determination you can start in that area, maybe in the pits or the team office from where you can start to climb and on a Monday morning you would feel happier to go to work because you are in an industry you want to be in. Think of the top job in the area in which you would like to work, supposing you like ballet, okay you probably won't ever get to be a ballet dancer but wouldn't it be better for you to be working as, say, a wardrobe assistant for a ballet company than an assistant in a supermarket warehouse.

I presented a radio programme for the BBC for many years but I didn't apply for a job as a presenter because I knew the chances of landing a job like that were virtually impossible for someone like me with no experience in the medium, apart from the odd interview I'd done over the years, but that would hardly qualify me for a presenters job. So I offered to work in the studios for no money, answering the telephones, running errands and so on, in fact I was prepared to do anything so long as I was in the area I wanted to be in and on the first rung of the ladder. I worked for just one day every week fitting it in around my other commitments with my usual job. I knew I was in the right place to learn about how radio works and more particularly how presenters went about their work. It also gave me the chance to get to know the people who might be able to help me gain the job I really wanted. Eventually I was asked to contribute small items on air, and after a while this became a regular occurrence, so there I was another step or two up the ladder. After proving to the management I could become a   competent broadcaster it was only a matter of time before one of the regular presenters went sick or off on holiday and I was asked to deputize for the absent presenter. I suppose I must have done the job to the required standard because I was now asked to deputize on a fairly regular basis, and was now being paid for my work. A few months after this I was at last asked to become a regular presenter with my own programme, which was to run for thirteen years. During this period I was asked to write and present for various BBC stations. So in all from offering my unpaid services it took me around four years to reach the top of my ladder. If I had wanted my future career to be in broadcasting I could have tried to climb even higher up the ladder, maybe becoming a producer, senior producer, or maybe on to higher management, but I knew my career didn't lay in radio management and was therefore happy on the step I had climbed to.

Life is all about climbing the ladder one step at a time. Whether it is the career ladder, the relationship ladder, the health ladder or even the financial ladder, they are all there from the time you are born just waiting for you to start climbing.

CHAPTER SEVEN

LAUGH YOUR WAY TO SUCCESS

How can a smile and a laugh help in improving your life and make you the success that you've always wanted to be? It sounds crazy doesn't it? A laugh is just something we do when we hear a gag and a smile is what we do when the gag isn't quite that funny, or when we meet a friend. Well you will no doubt be surprised to hear that both a smile and a laugh are very important elements of my BUSY method. Not only that, they are also a very important, not to say an essential, part of life in general. If we couldn't laugh or smile us humans would be doomed as a race, in a couple of centuries we would probably die out completely.

So are laughter and smiling just a reaction to a gag or flippant remark, or, in the case of a smile something we invariably do when greeting someone. Or could they be something that we are conditioned to do from birth for some deeper psychological reason. Because they are something we do automatically, in most cases, we tend to take laughing and smiling as something of little, if any, recognizable meaning, just a reaction to another persons action or words. They are, though, not only a major part of what differentiates humans from animals but are also one of, if not the most vital, constituents of my BUSY method. Without laughter and indeed a smile the method would be weakened which would increase the time a participant would need to change the way they use their brain, an essential part of the BUSY method.

In this chapter we must look at the reasons for laughter and smiles and explain why they are so essential to our happiness and wellbeing.

Let us start with the smile, why we smile and how it affects our brains and personality. In ancient man smiling wasn't a pleasant or happy action. In fact it was the exact opposite, a form of aggression. Much the same as we see today with members of the ape family, who bare their teeth in the form of a grin to show their anger or to challenge a potential enemy. In those far off days your teeth were your weapons, possibly the only weapons available to early humans, and showing your teeth to another human was tantamount to showing your weapon to anyone who challenged you or your position in the tribe.

Over the centuries this has slowly evolved into a show of happiness or politeness. It has also become a way of bonding with people. You meet someone, you smile and this shows that you are friendly towards them and mean them no harm, they smile back and a bond is formed. We all need to smile many times per day as it helps us feel good, it doesn't matter if we have nothing to smile about, a fake smile is as good for you as a genuine smile, the brain cannot tell the difference between a fake smile and a genuine one. The psychological effect on your brain is the same no matter that the smile is genuine or not. When you smile various things happen. First of all nerve cells send signals which travel from the brains cortex to the brainstem and from there the cranial nerves send the signal onwards to the muscles each side of the face that create a smile. However, when we activate a smile it sends a signal back to the brain, which stimulates reward mechanisms. In other words a smile makes us feel happy.

First thing in the morning, when you awake smile, for a few seconds, no matter how you feel, it really will make you feel better and put you in a positive frame of mind. According to statistics the average person smiles twenty six times per day but should smile much more than this, if you really want to achieve all the many benefits that a simple smile can bring. I realize of course that many people will say they can't walk around all day with what they think is a silly grin on their face but just think how many times you look in a mirror every day, to check your hair etc. If every time you do this you smile or whenever you read something nice or see a happy photograph in the press, online or something on television, just give a smile. Scientists have proved that a smile makes you feel better about yourself. The simple act of smiling can do so much more for us apart from showing our appreciation of a joke or a kind comment on meeting someone. It is in fact so much more than just an expression of happiness or gratitude.

When we smile we are exercising our smile muscles, they are called the Zygomaticus and are positioned either side of our nose in the cheeks. Even trying to pronounce the word should make you smile. Some smile research was carried out by scientists at Wuppertal University in Germany where they found that actuating the Zygomaticus muscles does not only improve your mood but this in turn reduces our food cravings while frowning on the other hand increases our cravings. So possibly a few quick smiles can also be part of your diet plan.

It makes no difference what your mood is, bored, depressed, or just feeling generally unhappy, smiling will release feel-good hormones called endorphins into your brain. These endorphins are the body's natural pain killers, that can either enhance or reduce how the body is feeling. They can also lower the heart rate, protect against infection, speed up recovery times and even help lower the level of the hormone cortisol, which is also known as the stress hormone, thereby lowering any stress levels you may be feeling.

There has recently been extensive research carried out by the University College London, and it was discovered that the more you smile the generally happier you were and this is what resulted in healthier and lower levels of cortisol. It has also been found that high levels of this hormone can substantially raise the risk of high blood pressure as well as increasing the risk of type 2 diabetes. So smiling is an important factor to enjoying a healthier lifestyle.

Even more important than that is the amazing discovery that smiling, together with a positive outlook on life, can mean that you are likely to live for longer. This comes from a year long study that was carried out at the Wayne State University, based in the Midwestern state of Michigan in the USA. It was during this research, into the ageing process, that experts studied photographs of over two hundred baseball players. The photographs were taken in 1952, and were published in the official Baseball Register. At the same time details were taken, and listed in the register, of all the players statistics, their date of birth, height, weight, marital status and so on. The researchers then compared the photographs with how long the one hundred and eighty four players, who had since died, had lived for. Their findings showed that the average life span of the players in the photographs who were not smiling was 72.9 years. Whereas the life span of the players who were just about smiling in the photographs averaged 75 years. However the players with a full smile, which is known as a duchenne smile, lived for an average of 79.9 years, a difference of 7 years between the non smiling players and the duchenne smiling players. Not a bad result for a simple smile.

It has been noted that a large percentage of the public rarely smile. They go about their daily lives with a grim look on their face as if the world is a dark and dismal place that they'd rather not be in. As if life is one long struggle through a dark tunnel until reaching their inevitable death. What a dreadful outlook this would be. Life is a wonderful journey with many rewards along the way and if yours isn't like this then that is your fault because you can and should do something about it and that should start with a smile. It is also noted that the official statistics state that the average person smiles twenty six times a day. Given that most people are up and about for sixteen hours a day, leaving the other eight hours for sleep, and that the average smile lasts for less than five seconds, most people smile for just over two minutes per day. Being the average number of smiles per day means that some people smile a lot more while others obviously smile a lot less. This really is a dreadful realization when you consider all the good that a smile can do for us.

We must all increase the number of times we smile each day. This is very easy to do if you follow a few simple rules. Start your day, every day, with a smile when you first wake up in the morning and you'll find it will put you in a better frame of mind to face the day ahead. It will also help you think in a more optimistic way banishing more negative thoughts. When you walk into the office smile when you say good morning to your colleagues. If you go to the supermarket smile at the cashier as you reach the checkout and you will find she, or he, will smile back at you, so you have not only helped yourself towards your daily quota of smiles but also the cashier.

Smiling is known to be contagious so if you give someone a smile you are not only making yourself feel happier, it is having the same effect on others. There are many other times during your day when you can raise a smile. When you look in the mirror smile and you will like better what you see. When you hear a piece of music that brings back good memories again give a smile. Lastly at the end of the day when you climb into bed smile for a few seconds before you switch off the light. This will help you sleep better because it promotes a feeling of contentment, relaxes you and prepares the body and, more importantly, the mind for a good night's sleep.

A recent study published in the journal Psychological Science reported that certain words we say automatically trigger a smile. There are different facial reactions to different words. Words such as, happy, smile, laugh, and funny all automatically generate a smile, whereas words like, bad, frown, annoyed, and depressed have the opposite effect.

Another piece of good news is that a smile is also an instant facelift. When you smile it plumps up the cheeks and gives a sparkle to the eyes. You might have noticed in the press and magazines whenever there are before and after photographs, usually advertising a beauty treatment or creams that are supposed to banish wrinkles, in the before photograph the model is almost always unsmiling, in the after photograph, after the beauty treatment, the model is always smiling as it lifts up the cheeks which has the effect of making the face look younger and brighter.

So smile and you will feel happier, look younger and possibly live longer, now that cannot be a bad thing. You have nothing to lose so smile much more every day and see the difference it makes to how you feel and how you look.

So smiling is much more important than we thought but laughing is even far more important to the body, the brain, our general wellbeing and of course the BUSY method. Laughter is the component of the greatest significance in the journey to unlocking your life and getting everything you ever wanted from it. This is the secret of it all that you will rarely hear about. Certain people know the secret of laughter, they are invariably very successful, very happy and always optimistic people. Learn to laugh and you will learn the secret to a successful life. Put it together with the other components of the BUSY method and you have the means to make your life happier and more successful that you could ever have imagined. It will also allow you to ask for and receive anything you desire because laughter puts you in a more positive frame of mind which will enable the law of attraction to work more effectively, but more of that later.

If you were to look up the word laughter in the dictionary it will tell you that it is, "to emit explosive, inarticulate, vocal sounds expressive of amusement, joy or derision". That explanation makes a laugh sound not much different to a belch but it is so much more than that. Laughter is born with us, a baby has to be taught to walk, talk, etc. but doesn't have to learn, or be taught, how to laugh, it is an instinctive action and is part of a universal vocabulary. Even though you may not be able to speak or understand another language, every person, no matter where in the world they come from, every culture, every creed, understands the meaning of laughter.

Scientists still have a lot to learn about the human brain and it's mechanisms that enable us to laugh but they are now learning just how beneficial it is to the human body and the mind. Just as a smile is contagious so is laughter, in the same way as the act of yawning is. When one person starts yawning others soon join in, and so it is with laughter, it only needs one person with a loud laugh to start laughing and soon everyone is laughing with them. The celebrated American author and poet, Ella Wheeler Wilcox, born in 1850, was among the first to recognize just how contagious laughter is when in 1883, on her way to the Governors inaugural ball in Madison, Wisconsin, wrote the opening words to her most famous poem, Solitude; they are:

"Laugh and the world laughs with you; cry and you cry alone."

Another quote from this same author that is so pertinent to our subject and how much determination plays in getting everything you want out of life is:

"There is no chance, no destiny, no fate, that can circumvent or hinder or control the firm resolve of a determined soul".

A baby is around three to four months old when it first discovers laughter and it lasts our whole life through, no matter what happens with the rest of our brain or our body, what we forget or what we physically can no longer do, we are all able to laugh until the very last breath leaves our body. Even people in the final stages of dementia who have forgotten their friends and family and even who they are, do not lose the ability to laugh, although of course whether they have reason to is another matter. Laughter evolved from the panting behavior that our primitive ancestors indulged in when in a happy or playful frame of mind. Certain primates of the ape family still make this panting sound when tickled or indulging in play fights with other apes. This, scientists believe is their form of laughter, it is only humans who vocalize laughter with ha, ha, ha, or similar sounds. Scientists and researchers now consider laughter to be so important and indeed essential to the wellbeing of both our minds and bodies that over the past few years there have been many clinics, clubs and societies opening up all over the world promoting laughter therapy in various forms. In Britain since 1991 the National Health Service has been running laughter clinics, so convinced are they of the benefits.

Indian cardiologist Madan Kataria after much research into the health benefits of laughing, opened his first laughter club in Mumbai at the beginning of 1995, where he teaches laughter yoga to hundreds of eager participants. At the time of writing there are now over eight thousand clubs spread over sixty five countries including fifty seven in Britain and the number is rising rapidly every year as more and more people realize just how beneficial laughter can be.

To check just what the benefits of laughing can be on our general and psychological health, Australian researchers showed a selection of patients comedy films. As they watched, the researchers monitored their health and responses throughout the sessions. The results showed that as well as giving the lungs and chest some good exercise, the laughter generated by the films gave the participants the same benefits as ten minutes of jogging.

Way back in the 1950's scientists discovered that people laughed for an average of eighteen minutes a day, now, in the twenty first century, we only laugh for an average of a mere six minutes per day. Could this be contributing in some way to the obesity crisis and the general increase in depression and anxiety problems reported by health practitioners? If so the remedy is simple and there will plenty more work for the laughter clinics to do.

But what if we don't want or don't have the time to go to a laughter clinic. We already know that a false smile can have the same effect as a genuine smile, so does the same thing apply to laughter? If it does can we just laugh at nothing at home alone, in other words give a fake laugh, and get results? The answer to that is a definite yes.

For a start laughter can do many of the things that a smile can do but in a far more intensive way. As we have heard laughter gives the lungs and chest a good workout, and regular laughter, similar to a smile, improves the immune system and releases endorphins, which are not only the body's natural pain killer but are thought by scientists to be up to thirty times more powerful than morphine. Research also shows that regular sessions of laughter encourage the body to clear out toxins, which can help improve the digestive system.

An intensive study was carried out by doctors and scientists, from the University of Leeds School of Healthcare, in which patients who suffered from serious leg ulcers were studied for five years to see what, if anything, could help cure or at least control their condition. The findings of this long research programme showed that laughter stimulates the diaphragm and therefore plays a vital part in moving the blood supply around the body. This in turn, they found, actually speeded up the patient's recovery, or in some cases improvement, from the leg ulcers. This research was reported in the prestigious British Medical Journal, which stated, "Forget technology, the best prescription for patients with venous leg ulcers is good quality nursing care and the occasional belly laugh." Just one more example of how laughter can help with healthcare.

More examples of the use of laughter in healthcare are being published in medical journals all the time, as in this one from doctors based in Basel in Switzerland. They discovered that regular bouts of laughter can often, help patients who suffer from chronic obstructive pulmonary disease by reducing hyperinflation. While doctors in Japan have recently discovered that laughter can greatly improve bacteria in the gut in people who suffer from eczema and so helped control the condition in 80% of the people who took part in the trial. Scientists, doctors and researchers from all parts of the world are beginning to find more and more benefits of the simple act of laughing. At the University of Athens researchers there found that laughter can reduce arterial stiffness and therefore can almost certainly improve artery function, thereby lowering the risk of heart disease as well as heart attacks. While in America at the College of Cardiology, doctors found that a good hearty laugh every day can, in most cases, reduce allergy symptoms by boosting the chemicals in the patient's bodies that block the release of histamine. Diabetic patients also receive help from having a good giggle, as it has been found to improve blood sugar levels as well as increasing good cholesterol in the body.

Yet another study of the good effects of laughter, this time at Oxford University in England, showed that after watching some comedy films and enjoying a good laugh, the participant's pain tolerance was heightened. We also know that laughter gives our hearts and lungs a very healthy workout whilst lowering blood pressure and at the same time increasing euphoria and releasing hormones into the blood stream, which help strengthen the immune system.

So seriously are the therapeutic benefits of laughter being taken by scientists and doctors based all around the USA they have set up the American Association for Therapeutic Humor. The aim of which is to enable members of the association to commission more research into the effects of humour and different kinds of laughter. So far they have compiled over one hundred studies that endorse the positive effects of laughter.

It is not just our general health or help with combatting various conditions and diseases, there are many other benefits we can all get from a good laugh, it can also help us lose weight.

Naturally enough as you would expect doctors to differ slightly in their conclusions on how laughter helps us to lose weight, but one fact they all agree on is that around fifteen minutes of laughter each day would burn off about forty calories. That is equal to a weight loss of up to five pounds per year for the average person. People who participated in one study carried out in Nashville, Tennessee, were found to have a ten to twenty percent higher energy expenditure when laughing at comedy films than during rest periods. The researchers discovered that laughing for fifteen minutes per day will use the same amount of energy as would a half mile walk. So staying at home and laughing for fifteen minutes while someone else has a brisk walk around town, for the same length of time, could have the same effect on both of you.

After exhaustive studies the doctors have stated that if a person can manage to laugh for an hour a day they would lose around 11lbs a year and laughing for an hour burns as many calories as 30 minutes of weightlifting. So the next time somebody says, "You're having a laugh mate". Just tell them, "Yes it's part of my diet plan".

On an even brighter note we are assured, by scientists, that laughter can in fact be an aphrodisiac. Several scientists carried out various surveys on many dating sites where they found that 88 percent of women put a sense of humour before good looks on their list of requirements. This fact is backed up by stories we have all heard and read about in the press many times about how a fairly ordinary looking guy gets the prettiest girl because he makes her laugh.

I have mentioned many of the health benefits of laughter but perhaps the longest and most thorough, study, was carried out by the Nord-Trondelag Health Study Group, in Norway. This research was spread over a fifteen year period and involved fifty thousand men and women who were assessed for their sense of humour. The scientists concluded that living a longer lifespan could be, to a large extent, down to laughter.

The thousands of people taking part in the study were tested multiple times over the fifteen year period and it was found that deaths due to cardiovascular disease were sixty three per cent lower in women with a good sense of humour and death from infectious disease in both men and women was around seventy five percent lower for people with a well defined sense of humour and therefore more likely to laugh for substantially longer periods. The scientists involved in the research for this, fifteen year, study concluded that a good sense of humour coupled with the laughter it causes has the effect of boosting the immune system substantially which in turn neutralized the effects of stress thereby extending the lifespan as well as the quality of life.

The brain of course is the key to my BUSY method and the power it contains to improve your life and enable you to achieve anything you aim for. We have seen what laughter can do for your health and wellbeing, making you happier as well as healthier. So what exactly does laughter do for the brain? It has recently been discovered that it can improve the memory, something that most of us could do with. Researchers into the effects of laughter on the brain found that people in their fifties and sixties who watched comedy videos for just twenty minutes had a measurable improvement in their memory of 43.6%. That is quite a big improvement so how does it manage to do this? Well it does it by reducing the levels of cortisal, a hormone that has been proved to impair learning and memory. If the levels of cortisal are too high they have been linked to the gradual loss of the connections between brain cells, which are known as synapses, in the prefrontal cortex. This is the part of the brain that contains the short term memory. Synapses help the brain to store as well as recall information. It is a well known fact among scientists that during and because of the aging process repeated exposure to cortisal can cause Synapses to slowly start to break down and eventually disappear thereby causing age related memory loss.

The world today seems to be run at a far faster pace than a few years ago. We used to send letters that took a few days to arrive at their destination, today we send emails that arrive in a second or two.

Motorways mean we drive at seventy miles per hour rushing through the journey as quickly as possible to keep to our, often imaginary, deadlines. Before motorways drivers were forced to take their time because of all the twists, turns, hills and roundabouts along the route, which also gave them more time to admire their surroundings. Today there's not much to admire on motorways even if we weren't going too fast to notice.

At work in factories and offices everyone is given targets that must be met, targets that are forced ever higher and with less time allowed. Delivery drivers are given minute by minute instructions and told the minimum number of deliveries they must make each hour, a total that seems to increase week by week. Mothers rush to drive the children to school in time then rush off to work, after which they rush back home, picking up the children from the child minders on the way, before cooking dinner for the family when father rushes home from a stressful day at the factory or office after trying to reach almost impossible targets. Rush, rush, rush, in seemingly ever decreasing circles when eventually, and not entirely unexpectedly, some will give way and suffer burn out or breakdown and visit the doctor who rushes through his day trying to minister to his ever increasing tally of patients.

Is it any wonder that the brain becomes stressed which will inevitably effect the way we think and act. The answer in many cases is simple, a good and regular dose of laughter will increase the production of serotonin which in turn creates endorphins. These will give the brain a boost to help reduce stress and the result is a more positive attitude, which will greatly help us cope with the, day to day stresses. One thing we mustn't forget is that apart from all the health benefits of laughter it also makes us feel happier and when we are happy we are naturally more optimistic and therefore less negative in our thoughts and actions. This means our brains are filled with positivity and it is this positivity and the way we use it that forms yet another vital component of my BUSY method

Chapter 8

BEING POSITIVE WHAT DOES IT MEAN?

The dictionary definition of 'positive' is, 'qualities expressed clearly or in a confident manner. Positive thinking, also known as Positive Psychology, enriches everyone's life with emphasis on personal growth and therefore happiness and becoming happy through positivity is a valuable asset. Being positive, or negative is a choice. We can all choose which way we want to go, choosing to be positive will mean that you will find your life is much happier and it becomes easier to get good results from challenging situations which effect us all from time to time. The more you practise positivity the more benefits you will get from it.

Inner happiness is the fuel of success.

Positivity is very powerful, not only does it help you get on in any area you have chosen to advance in, it will also help you handle the bad days and disappointments that inevitably encroach in your life from time to time. Being a positive person is not just how you are born, nobody is born positive or negative it is something you choose to be, anyone can change their mind set from being a pessimist to becoming an optimist and thereby avoiding negativity by being a positive thinker. The power in your thoughts is immense it is what makes your life what it is. Change your thoughts and you can change your life. Some eminent people believe we only use 10% of the power contained within our brains, although other, equally eminent, people consider this a myth. However the fact remains that, whatever your viewpoint, what we do know is that few of us use our brains to there full capacity. By training yourself to be a positive thinker you will use your brain far more productively than ever before.

Being positive is trying to always eliminate negative thoughts and actions and replacing them with the opposite. In most cases there is something positive to be found in everything that at first glance appears negative. For example, you look out of the window and see that it is raining and you think, "Oh dear it's raining, and if I go out I'll get a soaking so I'll just have to stay in all day, how boring, I'm fed up ".

Now another view of the same situation, "It's raining, good that means I wont have to water the plants and it'll be good for the garden and as I can't go out it'll give me the chance to catch up on my reading or binge on that television series that I missed. That is approaching a negative situation in a positive way.

If you think of this as a challenge and try to find something positive in everything, no matter how small, you will, over time, find it becomes a natural process and you will see that eventually you will become a more positive person and start to see the world in a positive light. We have all heard the old saying, 'The glass is half empty or is it half full', both of course are true but the art of positivity is to see it always as half full and pay no attention to the fact that it is also half empty. By thinking this way you are not denying that the glass is half empty, all you are doing is making a conscious decision to see the positive rather than the negative. If you are a pessimist and always think of the worst in every situation, you know the sort of thing: you buy a lottery ticket but convince yourself you won't win because the odds against are too great. So then you have two choices, you either don't get into that situation, i.e. you don't buy a lottery ticket, or you can just be happy that by buying the ticket some of the money you paid for it is going towards helping various charities. Research has discovered that thinking in a positive way can actually create real value and lead to great improvement in your life skills. It is important that you trust in yourself and you will find that you can change from negative to positive.

The statesman and former British Prime Minister, during the Second World War, Winston Churchill, had a good view of the difference between a pessimist and an optimist when he said:

"A pessimist sees the difficulty in every opportunity: an optimist sees the opportunity in every difficulty."

Every body has set backs, its part of the process of becoming a positive success. When something happens that stops you in your tracks, accept that things like that will happen occasionally but tell yourself that you have the talent and the right attitude to overcome it.

Try to always see the good things in your life. If you say there is nothing good in your life you are, I'm afraid, wrong. It is just that sometimes we can't see the good for all the bad that surrounds it. If you are having a bad day take a few minutes to sit down and think of a few good things in your life no matter how small they may be. After a few sessions of doing this you will find that it becomes easier to spot the good things and to let go of the bad things. Yes you still recognize that there are bad things in your life but you should just accept them and then carry on concentrating on the good things. Don't keep thinking that you can't do it, you must trust yourself and your ability. Believe me anybody can do this and the more determined you are the easier it will be. Set yourself goals so that every day you can see how you are moving forward a step at a time towards a positive lifestyle. The biggest mistake most people make is not setting their goals high enough. So don't limit yourself, you can go for anything you can think of.

Whenever you read a newspaper or watch the news on television you will find that there are always more negative stories than positive. You can guarantee that by far the largest percentage of any news bulletin or newspaper coverage will be about bad, sad or mad events that have happened, are about to happen, or might happen. I have often wondered why this is so and I have come to the conclusion that it is the reason why so many people are pessimistic. They read or hear about so many negative stories that the negativity seems to seep into their brains, slowly but surely. The media love negative stories because they make a better story, in their opinion. We've have heard how a policeman helping an old lady across the road is not considered newsworthy and therefore wont get a mention in the bulletins, however if that same policeman were to push that old lady into the road it will get coverage because it's seen as a better story.

All the negativity needs to be eradicated from your mind and replaced with positivity. This doesn't mean that the negative thoughts, actions, stories etc. wont happen or that they don't register with you, they do, but you don't let them effect your life or way of thinking. Think of good things that you want to happen in your life not the bad things that might, or might not, happen. Think about being happy, healthy and successful and you will become so.

Positive thinking is sometimes seen as a concept that is a bit of a joke these days but there have now been so many scientific studies into the subject that have proved that just as a person being subjected to continuous negative thoughts can become pessimistic, so the opposite is true. A person who is subjected to positive thoughts becomes much more positive or optimistic. It doesn't matter what state your mind is in when you commence the process, or how pessimistic you are generally, the brain is so powerful that if you persevere with thinking positively you will change your brain and if you follow my BUSY method you will harness the power of your mind and take control of your life and get to where it is that you want to be.

Change your thoughts and you change your life.

It means training your mind to be positive in outlook. Always searching for the good things in your life and in other people and believe me everybody has some good things in their life. You will hear people say that nothing good ever happens to them, and in many cases they believe it. This is because they focus on all the annoying or bad things that happen in their day to day life and when something good happens they dismiss it as a fluke or sometimes the good things don't even register with them because they are focusing so hard on the negative side and their brain becomes swamped with negativity. Being positive is an emotional attitude that will train your mind to expect and get the good things out of life, whatever they may be.

Being positive attracts happiness and other positive thoughts, while being negative attracts more negativity. Negativity is an international disease, people in every country in the world suffer from it to some degree or other. However we must never forget that negativity breeds negativity and positivity breeds positivity and with a positive outlook anything can be achieved if tackled in the correct way. It says in the Bible 'As you sew, so shall you reap', a simple statement but so true. It still applies to life today and is certainly one of the main tenets of my BUSY method. It means, in other words:

You get out what you put in.

Even the most pessimistic among us can train themselves to be more positive. It can take time but once you have a positive attitude you will find it will enhance your whole life, how you think, how you act, how you affect other people and how other people react to you.

Positive thinking is not just being optimistic or telling yourself you are feeling good today. It's about adding real value to your life. Many recent studies have shown that being positive can have a real and lasting effect on all aspects of your health, work and personal life. There was research carried out by scientists in an American University the results of which were recently published in the 'Journal of Research in Personality', where a group of ninety undergraduate students were tested for positivity. The group was split into two smaller groups one of which were instructed to write about a very strong positive experience every day for three days. The second group wrote about another topic that was neither positive nor negative. Three months later the two groups were once again subjected to formal assessment where it was established that the group who wrote about positive experiences showed they had fewer illnesses and therefore fewer visits to the medical centre and felt far happier than the other group. Given that this experiment lasted for just three days, it shows the intense power of positivity.

BELIEVE IN YOURSELF.

The secret to becoming a truly positive person is to believe you can do it. Without self-belief you will find it very difficult if not impossible to change. If you have no belief in yourself and therefore think it is not possible for you to become more positive, then to change this mindset is your first and most important task. The law of attraction states, 'Whatever you believe in you will get'. To start, take a pad and write a list of all your good points, your attributes, even if you can only think of one or two, it is important that you list them. Everybody has some good points no matter how pessimistic they are, think about them every day and write them down. You could start with simple statements, "I have nice eyes," or, "I get on well with people," "I am good with my finances." Don't worry if you can only think of one or two, tomorrow you will think of another one or two to add to your list and after a while you will have a comprehensive list which you should read every day and after a while you will have a much more positive impression of yourself.

Now start another list this time a list of what you can do, what you have achieved in your life so far. For example, "I can drive a car, I can cook, I can decorate a room," etc. Work on that list over a few days so you end up with a list of your attributes and your talents. Keep this list safe and when you have doubts about yourself read it again and gradually you will realize that you have increased your self-belief no end.

Now that you have belief in yourself you need to learn about positivity. Being a more positive person will bring happiness and attract other positive people. When people realize that you are a positive person your positivity and happy nature will effect them as well, so you are not only helping yourself you are helping other people. Start the journey by attempting to find a positive side to a negative news item. When you read about something bad in the

74

newspapers or see it on the television, think about it and try to find a positive side to the item, no matter how small. The more you do this the easier it will become although it will not always be possible of course especially when you hear about some of the dreadful events happening around the world these days. However you will find that after a while of looking for positivity in thoughts, news stories and life in general, it will become more natural to see the positive side until eventually your mindset changes and your brain accepts that you are now a positive, and therefore happier person and it becomes more powerful in the way you want it to act. This will not only affect your relationships with other people, colleagues at work, friends in your social circle, it will also make you a far more confident person and more able to make the right decisions that will lead to you getting all you want out of life.

If you have a bad day when everything seems dull, boring and nothing seems to be working as it should, which happens to all of us from time to time, don't start to doubt yourself and begin to think that you can't do it. Read your list of attributes and talents again and use this set back to make you even more determined to succeed. Dale Carnegie, the author of what is considered by many to be one of the first self-improvement books, written in 1936 and still selling today, titled 'How to Win Friends and Influence People', wrote the following:

MOST OF THE IMPORTANT THINGS IN THE WORLD HAVE BEEN ACCOMPLISHED BY PEOPLE WHO HAVE KEPT ON TRYING WHEN THERE SEEMED TO BE NO HOPE AT ALL'.

Quotes like this can play an important part in your journey as they can provide vital inspiration to help you forge ahead when you are beginning to falter. It is quite natural to have doubts or bad days as you go along this journey but when this happens to you consult you list of talents and attributes, listen to a favourite song or piece of music that brings back memories of a good experience in your life and you will find the doubts will begin to fade and the positive feelings return.

'THINK POSITIVE AND POSITIVE THINGS WILL HAPPEN'.

It has been known for a long time that positivity attracts positivity, just as negativity attracts more negativity. It's called 'The Law of Attraction', like attracts like, so it follows that the more positive you are in both thoughts and deeds the more positivity you will attract. There is no limit to what you can attract, everything you think of, good or bad, will attract more of the same. This is why when you wake in the morning with a doom-laden mind, thinking of something negative or bad in your life, everything else during the day seems to follow suit and you have a bad day. Likewise if you get up feeling positive and happy about the day ahead you will find the whole day becomes positive and happy.

'YOU ARE ONLY LIMITED BY YOUR OWN FEARS AND INACTION'

This is very true and applies to most of us at times. How many times have you thought to yourself, "I can't do that so why bother trying", or "I know I won't get that so there's no point in asking". Fear of failure and the subsequent inaction will stop you getting many things that you could probably have got if only you had conquered your fear and acted. We can't succeed in everything we try, sometimes we are not meant to succeed because what we are trying for is not right for us, but even if you do try to achieve something and fail, you will still have learnt a valuable lesson that you can put to good use next time you try for something.

Think positive, act positive and believe in yourself, because when you believe in yourself it will happen. Use my BUSY method as set out in the following chapters and I will prove that you can have the kind of life you never thought possible.

CHAPTER 9

You will have read the term, 'Law of Attraction' a few times in the previous chapters and indeed there are whole books written on this subject and it forms an important part of my BUSY method. So what exactly is the Law of Attraction? The Law of Attraction let's you see that you have total freedom and ability to take control of how your future develops.

It has been known about for thousands of years but can best be described by the sayings:

'LIKE ATTRACTS LIKE' 'YOU GET OUT WHAT YOU PUT IN'.

I have written earlier that the brain does a lot of work without us realizing it. I've mentioned things like breathing and making our other organs do their work when needed, without any conscious input from us. Even if we don't understand it, the law of attraction is responsible for bringing positive and negative influences that affect all our lives continuously. If you send out negative thoughts you will get negative thoughts back and likewise positive thoughts attract more positive thoughts. This being so it is vitally important to learn to minimize negative thoughts and actions and maximize positive thoughts and actions because how you think and act will have a very intense impact on your future life. If you focus on all the things that have gone wrong in your life you will only attract more things to go wrong. If you worry about what might go wrong in the future nothing is more certain than that more things will go wrong. You must learn to control or even get rid of negative thoughts and take control of your mind, fill it with positive thoughts and try to find positivity in negative thoughts. The law of attraction affects your health, finances, ambitions and relationships. Take health for example, in a previous chapter I wrote about the Placebo effect, which, nobody now doubts, has a great effect on all kinds of illnesses and conditions. People believe it will help them and it does and even when patients doubt that it can help their condition the brain takes over and works towards a cure because they tend to believe what the doctor tells them and this overrides their doubt. This is a version of the law of attraction and can be used in all other areas of your life. The law or versions of it are mentioned in the bible, for example, in Mark chapter 11, verse 24 it states:

"Therefore I tell you, whatsoever you ask in prayer, believe that you have received it, and it will be yours."

Remember, the power of prayer is really putting your thoughts into words. There are other examples quoted in other religious tracts throughout the world. In 1910 Wallace Wattles in his book 'The Science of Getting Rich', claimed that the law stems from the monastic Hindu view that God provides everything and can deliver anything that we focus on, and in 1907 author Bruce MacLelland, in his theology book, Prosperity Through Thought Force, summarized the law as:

" You are what you think, not what you think you are."

It is the belief that anyone can empower themselves to change their life and gain anything they desire and has been proved to work by many people over the years. Read my chapter on people who gained success despite the odds against and you will see how the law of attraction made it possible for them to overcome the odds and gain the success they wanted. Charles Haanel, in his book 'The Master Key System' wrote:

"The Law of Attraction will certainly and unerringly bring to you the conditions, environment and experiences in life, corresponding with your habitual, characteristic, predominant mental attitude."

Gradually over the years, quantum physicists have begun to realize the incredible power we all have within our mind and how it can affect our lives and the world we live in. Everything that has happened in your past life and everything that will happen in the future has been, and will be manufactured by your mind. This may not be an easy thing to accept especially if your life has so far not been good but it is the view of many that what we think about, if we focus, becomes reality. In other words focus on what you want, see it in your minds eye and it will become your reality. In 'The Power of Your Subconscious Mind', Joseph Murphy states:

"Readers can achieve seemingly impossible goals by learning how to bring the mind itself under control".

It cannot be emphasized enough just how much power is contained in the human brain, most of which of which we choose to rarely if ever use. The brain has the power to draw in energy from the universe, either positive or negative energy and it is up to us which we focus on and use. Most people's lives are too full of negative energy but this can be eliminated or at least minimized by having an optimistic attitude, determination and the ability to focus on positive vibrations which we send out to the universe. The law of attraction states that whatever we give out is returned to us. So if we give out positive energy we will attract the same energy back into our lives. Too often negative thoughts of hate, envy, resentment, anger and jealousy enter our mind and we must try to eliminate these and replace them with positive thoughts. To do this we have to take control of our mind and use it to our advantage. The author Napoleon Hill published 'Think and Grow Rich' in 1937, there are various accounts of how many copies of this book sold but they vary between 15 million and 60 million, so either way it is one of the best selling books of all time. In this book Hill says the importance of controlling one's thoughts cannot be overstated. Success comes from the way we use our mind, when we conspire to replace negative thoughts with positive and focus all of our attention on what we want to achieve, the universe takes over and makes it happen.

BE GRATEFUL BUT WHAT IS GRATITUDE?

Gratitude is our emotion that helps increase our ability to feel as well as express thankfulness and appreciation.

It is yet another of the vital components, along with the law of attraction, that makes my BUSY method so powerful. Never before has a self improvement method brought so many powerful components together in one, sure fire, way to gain success and a lifestyle many can only dream about.

If you are grateful for what you have and what other people give you, not only will that make you happier it will also make you a better person and have a positive effect on your friends, relationships and career, as well as helping you achieve your goals.

Having a grateful attitude makes you more optimistic about your life in general which in turn will help improve your health and therefore eventually your lifespan. Don't forget the law of attraction states that, 'what you give out, you get back', so being grateful for the thoughts and feelings that come from your friends, colleagues and the universe will bring kindness and happiness in return.

There are social, physical and psychological benefits of having a grateful personality. As well as providing you with heightened energy levels, it will greatly increase your satisfaction with life and reduce anxiety, stress and depression. It has even been found to help people recover from post-traumatic stress disorder by training patients to be grateful for what they have now rather that concentrating on the terrible things that they experienced in the past.

Being grateful for what you have, relaxes you and will help you get a better night's sleep and so allows you to wake feeling ready to face the world with a clear mind and a positive attitude. If you climb into bed with a mind full of worries the quality of your sleep will be nowhere near as fulfilling as if you go to bed thinking about things in your life that you are grateful for. Gratitude and a positive outlook are known to be one of the strongest relaxants available.

To sum up, gratitude will help improve your health, career, relationships, productivity, lifespan and happiness. Put this together with the other ingredients that go to make up my BUSY method and you are well on the way to a more successful and richer life than you ever thought could be achieved given your current circumstances.

A good way to start on the gratitude ladder, (remember that?) is to write down all the things you are grateful for. Now I know that lots of you are now saying, "I have nothing to be grateful for," but take a minute or two to think about it and you will find that we all have things in our lives to be very grateful for. Maybe your health, job, children, home, a good friend or even a beautiful view you have just seen, or a cup of coffee given to you by a good friend. When you start thinking about them others will spring to mind. Keep the list safe and try to add to it every day and when you are having a bad day or negative thoughts abound, pull out the list and study it for a few minutes and you will find that the negative thoughts will fade and you will be transformed into a more positive and happier frame of mind.

Studies have shown that no matter how negative you are, it is possible to train yourself to cultivate gratitude. Writing down things for which you are grateful every day and spending a few minutes studying them will boost your levels of enthusiasm and determination and therefore help you progress through the complete BUSY method.

Various research studies carried out at several universities have proved that our thoughts have all the necessary power to alter the way our brains work. We can change our brains from being mainly negative to very positive. I have shown in the early part of this book how we can condition our brains to believe that we are not worthy of a certain lifestyle. Remember the married couple who despite working hard throughout the years, decided that new cars and big houses were, 'not for the likes of us', and so they never did have new cars or a big house in a nice area because they had conditioned their brains to accept the fact that they would never get them no matter how hard they worked. Well we now know that that thought process will work just as easily in reverse. So when you study your gratitude list every day close your eyes for a few minutes, relax and concentrate on the things you are grateful for in your life and soon that gratitude will become embedded in your brain, changing it's way of working and the benefits will begin to materialize.

NOW VISUALISZE YOUR DESIRES

This probably sounds a little bit strange or weird even, as if visualization is some kind of magic. Believe me it isn't magic or hocus pocus, visualization is being able to see in your mind's eye the end result of what it is that you want. We all see things in our mind that we would like, perhaps we see ourselves laying by the pool in our holiday hotel. This though is just a snapshot, a single frame picture of what it is that we want. Visualization is seeing that image in far more detail as in a film of that desire. See yourself walking to the pool imagine feeling the sun on your face, seeing the other people you are about to join at the pool side, see and feel every aspect of your wishes. If, for instance, you want to get the top job in your work place, visualize it as if you already have that position and when you see and focus on this image, in every detail, of you as the top man in the job you will become more motivated to pursue and reach your goal.

Scientific research and the evidence gained from it supports this method of self-improvement which has been used for many years by successful people in all kinds of different careers. Boxing legend Muhammad Ali stresses in his autobiography and in many interviews how he visualizes himself having won the fight before it happens and has stated that visualization is a very important part of his preparation. We can use this technique to prepare for many situations, a job interview, a presentation, to achieve success in whatever field you are interested in, or to improve your performance in whatever way you wish. Visualization is a technique that has been used regularly by many successful business executives, all over the world, to help them focus on their goals and desires.

The secret is not to visualize what you want and just hope you can get it, or even to tell yourself, I will get it, it is to visualize that you already have the thing that you desire. To get the most out of visualization you must see that you already have whatever it is that you want. Obviously you know that this is not so but your subconscious mind cannot distinguish between the reality and what is imagined and will react to the images you create. That doesn't mean that you think of something and it happens immediately, it will take time and practise but it will happen.

Professor Aymeric Guillot P.H.D. from the Center of Research at the University Claude Bernard in Lyon, France, has found that if we imagine a difficult walk or actually do the walk the reaction of the nerve cells in the neural network is very nearly the same. This theory was tested in a study that was featured in the prestigious North American Journal of Psychology, a few years ago. Athletes were asked to imagine doing a series of hip-flexor exercises five times a week for fifteen minutes, while another team was tasked with actually performing the exercise on a weight machine. It was found that the strength gains of both teams were almost identical.

Another amazing example of the power of visualization concerns Natan Sharansky, a computer specialist who, in the 1980's, was accused of spying for the United States and sentenced to nine years in prison in the USSR. He spent most of his sentence in solitary confinement and in an attempt to pass the time he played himself in mental chess games. Obviously he had no chess board or pieces as the whole thing was played out in his mind. He played many games in his head while telling himself he would become a world-class champion. Despite never having been a professional chess player, after his release Sharansky beat the world chess champion Garry Kasparov, a perfect example of visualization and how it works.

As the examples above show, it has been known for some time that thoughts activate the same mental instructions as actions, so let it do the same for you. Focus on your goals and desires, see the end product clearly and it could be you enjoying your success or driving your new car, or even enjoying a meal with your new partner. Whatever it is picture it in your mind, focus on the picture, not just for a second or two, keep the vision in your mind and come back to it several times a day, seeing the picture in all its detail and your brain will start working on ways to make you reach your goal. It is your subconscious mind that will programme your brain to start working on ways to help you turn the thing you focus on into a reality.

Have you ever thought about someone you haven't heard from for a while, wondered how they are and what they are doing, then, within a very short time they call or a letter or email arrives from them? This is an experience most of us have had from time to time and we put it down to coincidence. In fact it is caused by a part of our brain called the recticular activating system, which creates solutions to many of your thoughts in the same way as when you go to bed trying to think of a solution to a particular problem you have been trying to work out without success and when you wake in the morning the solution, that you were unable to find the night before, just pops into your head. This has happened because your subconscious brain has searched for and found the solution to the problem while you were asleep. You had visualized the problem, focused on it for a while and your brain turned the vision into reality.

HOW TO PRACTISE VISUALIZATION

If you work your brain you will give a charge to your sympathetic nervous system. This will in turn increase your heart rate, blood pressure and breathing, in the same way as doing physical exercise will. The same thing happens when you are subjected to a very dangerous or frightening episode, the 'fight or flight' response automatically kicks in with the same effect on your heart rate, blood pressure and breathing. In other words you can get the same response whether visualizing something or physically doing it. If you visualize performing a task repeatedly your neural pathways will become conditioned to this and will enhance your motivation as well as your confidence in your abilities to succeed. When you visualize something that you want to achieve remember to see it in the greatest detail. You wont need to visualize it for hours on end but it will help to concentrate your mind if you get into the habit of visualizing your goals at roughly the same time every day for around ten minutes each time. The more detail and the more vivid the visualization the better and faster you will see the results begin to appear. On the other hand this will need practise, it is not something that most people can automatically do to any great degree. You will find that you can concentrate on something you want and after a few seconds another thought comes into you mind and clouds your visualization, but with practise you will learn to keep these other thoughts out and visualize the one thing you want. If you can't manage to visualize your goals then in most cases the chances of achieving them will be much diminished.

Many successful people have used and are still using visualization to achieve and continue their success. Golf champion Tiger Woods has claimed that he has been using it since before he was a teenager. World champion Jack Nicklouse has said he would never hit a shot without a very clear picture of how he wants it to go in his head.

Sara Blakely, was named the worlds youngest self-made billionaire by Forbes magazine in 2012. Founder of the Spanx, ladies underwear, company, her products can now be found in over fifty countries. Sara is a great believer in visualization and has said that:

"If you mentally see yourself in a scenario you'll start to make decisions in your life that get you there".

You must get very vivid pictures in your mind and the more focused you are the better the results and the easier it will become to block out the negative thoughts that will intrude now and then. Visualize the whole scenario, not just succeeding but also seeing what you will do with this success, your new clothes, new car, new house, how you feel having gained your goal, and this will increase your chances of becoming successful and the speed at which it begins to arrive.

When you visualize your future and the goals you wish to attain, if you practise, and perfect it, you are not just dreaming, visualization is a technique that is based on scientific evidence that has been proved to work for many successful people. It works through neurons in our brain that transmit information that tells our body to act in a certain way to pursue our imagined imagery in the same way it would to a physical goal or activity and achieves a similar result. It is a powerful way to achieve the means and ways of creating the path to the lifestyle that you desire.

So, practise visualization, harness the power therein and you will be well on your way to adding another component of my BUSY method that will soon put you in touch with the changes and desires you wish for yourself.

Chapter 10

GET ON WITH THE BUSY METHOD

We now have all the ingredients for the BUSY method, so all you have to do is mix the ingredients together to make the complete BUSY cake. I liken the method to a cake because putting all the components together is rather similar to baking a cake. You get the recipe but often one or two of the ingredients are not available or you forget to put them in. In this case you will still end up with a cake of sorts that is still possibly acceptable but it is not the same cake as in the recipe. It is the same with putting together the BUSY method, you can leave out one or two of the ingredients and you will end up with a version of the method but it will not be the version that I have recommended and have tried and tested. On the other hand if you were to leave out too many of the ingredients what you will end up with is something that is not my BUSY method and certainly won't work in the way that my method will.

Each ingredient, on their own, can be of help to you. For instance, becoming more positive cannot be a bad thing, and being grateful for what you have got can lesson stress and maybe make you a more contented person. However to get the real benefit from my BUSY method, and achieve anything or everything you want, you need to use all the components and learn to use them together in the correct way. Practise them regularly and you will get the results you desire. As with learning any new skill the amount of practise and the intensity with which you apply to the learning process will determine the time frame for the appearance and quality of the results. The BUSY method should be seen as more of a way of life rather than a quick fix method to change everything about your life and gain every material thing you ever wanted. Changes will continue to happen over time although many people have shown surprise at the speed with which some results can start to appear particularly in reducing stress levels and increasing general feelings of happiness and contentment.

Here is a reminder of the main components and what they will do for you as part of my BUSY method.

BELIEVE IN YOURSELF

Without belief in yourself and your abilities you have nothing. It was American minister and author, Norman Vincent Peale, who said:

"Believe in yourself. Have faith in your abilities. Without a humble but reasonable confidence in your own powers you cannot be successful or happy."

We all have doubts now and then but that is a common occurrence and is not the same as, not believing. You can start to train yourself to believe by writing a list of your attributes, and believe me we all have some. Take your time and as you think of something add it to your list. It could just be something very simple such as, 'I am good at cleaning the house', or 'I am a tidy person'. Over a day or so you will see how much the list has increased and when you start to see how many things you are good at or the positive things about your personality, for example, 'I am kind hearted', or 'I have a good attitude to my work', you will begin to believe that you are not such a bad person after all. Once you get to this stage start telling yourself that you can make a success of your life and you will make a success of the BUSY method.

PREPARATION AND DETERMINATION

These are really self-explanatory. Be prepared to concentrate on the various components and advice on how to use them to your best advantage, as laid out in the 'How to Use' chapter. Work out, when are the best times to fit in with your lifestyle, work commitments and so on. Make a plan of action and stick to it as much as possible so that it becomes routine.

We all know that the most important part of any job is the preparation and so it is with the BUSY method. The more preparation and planning you do beforehand, the easier and more successful the job will be.

Determination is also an important part of the success of the method. Tell yourself you will succeed often enough and within a short while your brain will come to accept this and start to work towards that end. Naturally there will be times when that determination will falter and you will begin to doubt the power of the method but in those moments you should get angry with yourself for doubting your abilities and the method and tell yourself that you can and will succeed and the BUSY method will get you there. Fight negative thoughts and they will appear less often and it will become easier for you to dismiss them when they do encroach on your consciousness. Your determination will become stronger the more you practise it. The more often you tell yourself that you will succeed the nearer to success you will become, until eventually your determination takes over completely and from then onwards you will know without a doubt that success is within your reach. Being determined trains your brain to act in the way it needs to make your success come to fruition.

GRATITUDE

One could be forgiven for saying, "What has gratitude got to do with getting everything I want?" "Of course I would be grateful after I have achieved everything, but gratitude for what I have before I start on the method?" "How will that help?"

The answer to that is that being grateful for what you have is very important because it will help your brain to see things differently and help you to focus on good thoughts instead of bad. If you are concentrating on all the things that you haven't got or aspects of your life that you are unhappy about you will use up valuable energy on thoughts that are of no use to you and certainly will not improve your life. The more you think about the negative things in your life the more you will attract. I am sure most of us have had the experience of worrying about how to pay that bill when it came in at the wrong time of the month. Then as you are wondering how best to pay it, other things that need money just seem to jump into your mind to join your original thought about the one bill. Before you know it your mind is full of all the things that have to be paid for, what needs repairing and so on, so the one thought attracted other similar thoughts. Now if that original thought had been gratitude, for the fact that you will be able to pay the bill at the end of the month, or for something else in your life then that will have attracted other grateful thoughts. This will not only make you feel better it will attract other good things into your life. If you are resentful, jealous, negative and all your thoughts are focused on what you don't have you will just attract thoughts of more and more things that you don't have or are unhappy about. Be grateful for what you have, even the smallest things, two hands to hold a new born baby, two feet to walk in the country with, two eyes with which to be able to see the sunshine on the garden and you will soon begin to attract and enjoy a grateful life and the rest of what you want to achieve will be attracted to you.

POSITIVITY

Being positive, like being determined and being grateful, is a learned attribute. The more you practise being positive the easier it will become. To start the process, try to find some positive angle to one of your negative thoughts. It might not spring to mind immediately but take a few minutes and you will find something positive in every negative thought or action. Even the tiniest bit of positivity will help to train your mind as well as giving you generally a much better outlook on your life, which you will find extremely useful when striving to achieve your goals.

Martin Seligman, known as the father of learned optimism, and author of many books on the subject, states:

"If you believe you are worthwhile and deserving of happiness, your view of the world around you and events that affect you will be positive."

Never doubt the power of positivity, it will instill confidence which in turn will enable you to see situations with an expectation of success. When a negative thought enters your mind, which it will do, even the most positive among us occasionally have these thoughts, deal with it immediately, the worst thing you can do is leave it to fester. If it is something that can be sorted out then do it at once. If it is just a negative thought about something that you can do nothing about, dump it and get on with your life. There is no worth in worrying about something that you cannot change. Being positive will not only make you a happier person it will enable you to see your future and where you want it to lead far more clearly. There are no benefits from being negative but the benefits from being positive are innumerable, why would anybody not want them as part of their life.

A LAUGH OR A SMILE MAKE IT ALL WORTHWHILE

A line from an old song but I suspect the writer had no idea just how beneficial a laugh and a smile can be for all of us, or what they can do for our health, wellbeing and attitude to, and ability to gain success. My method will teach you how to use laughter and the act of smiling as part of your daily routine to train your brain to work towards your goals.

It is all too easy to ridicule the simple act of smiling or enjoying a few laughs, but as I explain in previous chapters they can do an enormous amount of good, not only for the physical health of the individual but also the mental health and brain training needed for the BUSY method to work to its optimum level.

Laughter is something that is all to often left out of self-improvement and self-help books, but I include it because I know from past experience just how vital it is. Not only for building happiness and confidence but with increased happiness and confidence comes more determination and having practiced positivity as well, you would now be well on your way to achieving everything your heart desires.

So, with regular doses of laughter and smiles you become healthier, happier, more confident, more positive and more determined along with the many other benefits that laughter promotes. Laughter is arguably better for you than almost any pill or treatment on the market today. Do not ridicule or dismiss the importance of laughter because it will do more to get you where you want to be than any other component in my BUSY method. All the various components are important but laughter is the catalyst that will make everything work together and bring extraordinary power to the method.

THE LAW OF ATTRACTION

This is something that has been accessible to all of us forever. It is mentioned in ancient manuscripts and in the bible (Galatians chapter 6 verse 7.) where it says 'As you sew so shall you reap.' In other words, 'you get out what you put in'. The Law of Attraction states that like attracts like. It is not magic it is scientific fact although as with everything it has its deniers but then there are also global warming deniers and others who deny that the world is round and are certain in their own minds that the earth is flat, so there will always be believers and disbelievers. I am quite definitely a believer because it has worked for me many times over the years and continues to do so.

Have you ever woken up in the morning feeling a bit down, not looking forward to the day ahead and before you've left the house things have started to go wrong. Perhaps you stub your toe getting out of bed, burn the toast, go to the bathroom and find you've run out of toothpaste, and you immediately know that it is going to be one of those days when everything goes wrong, and so it turns out, one thing after another goes wrong throughout the day. Have you ever wondered why this happens? Think about it, one little thing goes wrong at the start of the day and you assume that other negative things will follow and sure enough they do. Its, like attracting like, which is the basis of the law of attraction.

On the other hand you might wake up feeling full of the joys of spring and the day goes really well, everything falls into place and for once it seems you can do no wrong. This again is the law of attraction working, you think good, positive thoughts and therefore attract more of the same.

We've all had experiences similar to those mentioned above, but what if instead of just letting your actions dictate your thoughts, you stub your toe and think the rest of the day will be bad, you concentrate on what you want out of life and let the law of attraction provide it. It won't necessarily work immediately, its unlikely you will think of a new car and one appears on your driveway, but that doesn't mean it is not working, if you focus on that new car often enough the law of attraction will show you the best way to obtain it. The law doesn't always make things appear in front of your eyes, although there are plenty of documented cases where this has happened. If, for instance, it is success at work that you wish for it will more often than not be a gradual process, it is unlikely that you will be the office boy one day and the managing director the next, but this will not stop you moving up the ladder rapidly. It is your thoughts that control what the law of attraction brings to you, if you think good, happy successful thoughts, then more of the same will come to you.

Often people will say to me that they have thought about wanting a new car every day and they still haven't got one. The answer to that is simple, remember, 'like attracts like', so if your thoughts are all about what it is that you want then more of what you want will come back to you. If your thoughts are about your new car, what it looks like, what it smells like, what it drives like, then it will arrive. Don't think about what you haven't got, imagine that you already own these things, think about them in detail, the way to make the law of attraction work at its most powerful is to use:

VISUALIZATION

Visualizing what it is that you want has the effect of strengthening the results from the law of attraction. See what it is you want in very great detail. If it's a new house visualize it, how does it look, imagine you are unlocking the front door, walking in, feeling the carpet under your feet as you walk on it, what does the furniture look like, imagine the lay out of the rooms, the colour of the walls and so on. If its success at work that you want, imagine yourself running the company, what are you wearing, how do your colleagues treat you, imagine your pay cheque, visualize the figures on your bank statement.

Seeing what you want in all its detail is in effect instructing the law of attraction to return that vision to you in reality. That is how 'like attracts like' works.

These seven components make up my BUSY method. All you need now to get started is to learn how to put them together and use them daily in the most productive way, then you will be on your way to realizing your dreams and becoming a much happier, healthier, wealthier and more successful person.

PART TWO

CHAPTER 11

GETTING STARTED

So now the time is right to get on with the BUSY method and start the journey to achieve everything you have ever wanted. As stated previously, preparation is the key to formulating the most productive plan that suits your day to day lifestyle whilst getting the best results from the method.

I will give you a basic plan to start you on your journey but before you start there is one thing to remember, you are in sole charge of your life, whatever you do or whatever you want is in your hands. I have said before this is not magic, it is how you use the parts of your brain that have so far been left almost dormant. There are so many thousands, if not millions, of more things the human brain can do for you to improve your life but most people live their whole life without realizing this. Your brain is just waiting there, suspended in a liquid called cerebrospinal fluid inside your head, it is waiting for you to start exploring and using the power within that most of us have never used before.

I was, for many years one of life's worriers. If I didn't have anything to worry about, I worried about it. Every morning I would wake up and the first thought to come into my head was a worrying one. Would I get to work on time? Would there be any more bills waiting for me on the doormat? What is that ache in my back, is it something serious? These were the type of thoughts that started my day and naturally more and more worries would come into my head during the day via the law of attraction. Then, at last, after years of a large percentage of my time spent worrying I realized that there is no need to live like this. There is no need for anyone to live in a constant state of worry and the misery it can cause. I now wake every morning excited about what the day will bring, and so can you. If using my BUSY method just makes you a happier person living a more fulfilled life of contentment then it will have been well worth the effort and the price of this book. Get your brain working as it is designed to, unlock your brain and you will soon find that you have unlocked much more, in fact you will have unlocked your life.

You can achieve everything your heart desires if you use my method correctly and methodically. It doesn't matter whether it's a better job, a new relationship, a new car or a new house, any, or even all of these things can be yours for the asking.

Anything worth having is worth working for, the more dedicated you are to the BUSY method, the more productive it will prove to be and the faster the results will arrive. I will lay out the method that I found suited me and that I still use every day even after all these years. Feel free to alter the order of things to suit your lifestyle but, for the best results, use all the components every time, preferably every day until it becomes a part of your daily routine. Firstly you will need to write one or two lists, the first of which I call:

THE DESIRE LIST

This is the list of everything you desire when you have finally unlocked your life. It doesn't matter how far fetched some of them may seem to you, write them all down and keep the list safe because you are going to use it most days. Do not write the list as things you want, for example, I want a new car, or I would like a new car, you must write it as if you already own it and write it in great detail, 'I have a brand new black BMW with tan leather interior' and so on. The more detail you put in the better the result. If it is success in your job that you require, write it as if you are already in that position and again add the details such as, where you work, what does your office look like, what salary you are paid. The reason we do this is because of the law of attraction, remember, like attracts like, so if you write "I want a new car or I want promotion at work', the law of attraction will bring you more of the same, in other words, more of what you want, instead of delivering those things to you. You can make the list as long as you want, include all your desires with as much detail as possible. It is best not to just scribble down a list on scraps of paper because you are going to use it often and don't want it to get lost or torn, so make the list as good as you can maybe writing it in a special note book that you keep by your bed or on your desk so that it is ready for you whenever you need it. Take your time in writing this list because it is your future and as such deserves to be treated with respect.

The second list you are going to need is what I shall call:

THE GRATITUDE LIST

It is very important to show and feel gratitude for what you have and what others give you. I don't mean just material possessions, you might be grateful for having a good sense of humour for example or good health or even for being able to see a nice view from your window. Friends may give you loyalty or honesty for which you are grateful. You will of course feel gratitude for the material possessions you have acquired over your life as well but it is essential that you write a comprehensive list in your note book because being more grateful and showing that gratitude to others will alter the way you look at your life.

If you show your gratitude for the little things someone does for you they will be pleased at your reaction and automatically feel that they want to do more for you. The same thing applies when a friend or colleague is grateful for something you have done or said, you will be happy to do more for them.

Write your list and study it often, add to it as more things happen that you are grateful for because as you go along, studying the BUSY method, you will become a more grateful person and that will attract more gratitude towards you. Not only will this make you a happier and nicer person it will bring all sorts of other rewards into your life. The power of gratitude should never be underestimated, it is one of the most powerful emotions available to us, so write your list and use it to help you achieve your aims.

So now that you have your two lists, which you will use along with the other components of the BUSY method but what do you do with them to help you get the best results? You do not have to use the method in the same way as I do. The way I use it suits my lifestyle but might not be suitable for yours so don't be worried about changing the routine that I lay out here, so long as you use all the components the order you use them in is not so important. Firstly it is important to remind yourself what BUSY stands for:

BELIEVE IN YOURSELF. UNLOCK YOUR MIND. SUCCESS IS YOURS.

Therefore you must start by convincing yourself that you can, and will succeed. The more you tell yourself you will succeed the easier it will become to believe in yourself and your desires. It can be likened almost to a form of self hypnotism. You need to have a positive outlook and you get that by keeping positive thoughts in your head and dismissing negative thoughts or in many cases just looking for the positivity within negative thoughts.

The best time of day to train yourself is when you are asleep. The brain works on two levels, the conscious and the subconscious, when we are asleep our brain is working solely on the subconscious level, therefore it can work on our wishes and how to achieve them for us without the hindrance of our conscious thoughts getting in the way. When we are awake we might think and visualize something we desire but as we are visualizing it negative thoughts creep in or things happen that disturb our train of thought and interrupt our visualization. However, if we think about and visualize whatever it is that we would like just before we fall asleep the brain can work on that desire without interruption while we sleep. When we are awake it is our conscious thoughts that control our lives and ambitions but asleep it is our subconscious thoughts that take over and our subconscious thoughts and more importantly the part of the brain that controls them, is far more powerful than when we are awake and the brain is working on it's conscious level because it has far fewer interruptions to disrupt the process.

Last thing at night spend a few minutes smiling. This might seem a rather futile exercise but believe me it works wonders. Smiling releases certain chemicals in your brain, which will make you feel happier and put you in the right frame of mind to visualize your desires. Spend a few minutes, each night, thinking about your aims and desires and visualize them as if you already have them. This will send you to sleep and let your brain work on those aims unhindered for the next few hours. Do this regularly every night and it will help keep you in a positive frame of mind and begin to find the necessary ways to realize your dreams.

Likewise when you wake in the morning smile for a few minutes to start your day as you want it to continue. In a previous chapter we discovered just how much good a smile can do for you so make it your mission to smile more often during the day. Most of us would automatically smile when we meet friends or colleagues throughout the day, but you also need to consciously smile more. Every time you look in a mirror smile at your reflection, when you sit down to eat smile before you start your meal and smile as you finish. This extra smiling will start to change your personality into a more positive one.

Start to see the positive side of everything, if a negative thought enters your head try to see it in a different way. If, for instance, a colleague or someone you encounter during the day is rude to you, instead of thinking about how rude they were, wondering why they behaved in that way to you and letting that negative thought fester in your mind, think instead how glad you are that they are no longer around so cannot be rude any more. Or tell yourself that they probably had something bad or stressful happen to them that put them in a bad mood. In other words give them the benefit of the doubt and think positive. With practise you will now be smiling more and becoming a more positive person.

The next step is to make time to read your list of things you feel grateful for. Find just five minutes or so each day to read through and think about how lucky you are to have these things to be grateful for. After a while of doing this it will become almost automatic that you go through your list and feel your gratitude. Close your eyes for a minute and let the gratitude you feel flow over you.

After a few weeks of taking these steps you will be happier, more positive and a more grateful person, not bad so far. These actions will have already altered the way your brain is working for you by bringing into use parts of it that you haven't perhaps used before.

We now need to get you laughing more because as we have previously stated in Chapter 7 it is one of the most important actions you can perform for yourself. If you are stressed laughing reduces the stress, if you are in a negative frame of mind laughter will make you feel more positive. There are of course laughter clinics available in many countries throughout the world, which you might like to use or there are laughter yoga classes held regularly in many towns, but if you can't or don't want to take part in these then you can increase your laughter quota in the privacy of your own home quite easily. Laughter does not even have to be genuine for you to feel the benefits. Watching comedy films or listening to comedy recordings might work well for some people but if you have no time or inclination for doing this try laughing alone for a few minutes several times during the day and this, you will find, will help the rest of the BUSY components work better and faster for you, as well as supplying all the other benefits mentioned in an earlier chapter. Choose a time and place that suits you to practise this, maybe instead of singing in the bath or shower try laughing, or as you clean the house or do the ironing, laugh as you do it. With a little thought and practise you will become adept at laughing throughout the day and the results will help make you a more positive, as well as a healthier and maybe even a little slimmer person. Laughter therapy works whether you go to group therapy sessions or practise alone at home. So don't be shy about it, laugh whenever and wherever you can and reap the benefits.

Now that you are feeling more positive and grateful the next daily task is to read through your list of desires and visualize each item as if you are already in possession of it. In your mind's eye see it in detail and see the results of having it. Feel the emotion of having all that you want. How you will feel, how you will act, how others will react to you now that you have everything you desire. You can sit back, close your eyes and visualize, as I suggest, last thing at night, but if you put a copy of your list somewhere you are able to see it as you go through the day, on your desk, pinned to your notice board or even stuck on the fridge door, you will be able to look at it and visualize your desires as you go about you daily routine. Visualize, visualize, visualize and your brain will subconsciously work on obtaining your desires and the law of attraction will do the rest for you.

Remember, believe in yourself and in the law of attraction, be determined and never give up. You can and will succeed.

Here is the list of BUSY components and the way I use them but as previously stated feel free to alter the routine to suit your lifestyle.

1:      Smile for a few minutes when you wake in the morning.

2:      Read and think about your gratitude list and say a silent thank you for all
the good in your life.

3:      Make time to laugh as much as you can throughout the day.

4:      Read through your list of desires and think about them during your day.

5:      Visualize in detail all your desires as many times as possible during the
day.

6:      Before going to sleep smile and visualize your desires in detail for a while
and make these thoughts your last before falling into sleep.

7:      Most important of all, Believe you can do it.

Practise these steps regularly and let the law of attraction work for you.

JUST SEVEN SMALL STEPS THAT WILL UNLOCK YOUR MIND.

CHAPTER TWELVE

Many people are reasonably content with most aspects of their life. Their relationship is good, their career is going the direction they would wish and generally they have good health. However most people have something in their life that they would like to change. Usually it involves a problem they have tried and failed to conquer several times before. I am often asked if the BUSY method can be used to make these problems easier to solve. I believe that the BUSY method can be used to enhance many already existing methods of solving some of the most common problems. So here are a few ideas to help with some of the most familiar problems people tell me they want to tackle using the BUSY method.

LOSING WEIGHT

In theory it is very easy to lose weight. Eat less and exercise more, we all know that but putting it into practise is not always easy. We know we should all be able to do this whenever we need to but there are just two little things stopping this method from working for us, willpower and peer pressure. We have all experienced it when trying to lose a few pounds. You might be doing quite well cutting out the cakes and chocolates, then you have a bad day when everything goes wrong at work, the weather is dreadful and there's a pile of bills in the morning post. You are walking round the supermarket searching for something tasty and filling, but containing very few calories, then you walk past the special offer on cream cakes. Well, one won't hurt will it, except they come in packs of four. Weakened by the day's events you give in, well they say you should treat yourself now and then. The trouble is after you have broken your diet once and convinced yourself no harm has been done, you start to treat yourself too often and before long the diet has gone out of the window along with your receding waistline.

So can the BUSY method help you to lose weight? The answer is, yes it can but there is no magic formula that will enable you to stuff yourself with cakes, burgers and booze and watch the pounds melt away. That is something that will not happen. So how can my method help? If you are serious about getting the weight off there are a few rules that must be followed, probably the most important one is:

DO NOT GO ON A DIET

Do not go on a diet when you want to lose weight might sound a ridiculous thing to say but think about it for a while and you will see why nearly all diets don't work in the long term. People go on a diet, cut out certain foods and alcohol and if they follow the rules start to lose weight. Eventually if you are lucky and determined you reach your target weight. Hooray! Now I have finished my diet and lost the extra pounds I wanted to and I can now eat normally again. Then, guess what? As soon as you start eating normally again, as you did before you started this miraculous diet, all the weight you lost plus usually a bit more goes back on faster than it came off.

The fact that you are on a diet means that one day you will finish it and that is when it, and you go pear shaped. Doctors and nutritionists will usually recommend that after you have reached your target weight you should go on a maintenance diet. Well that diet isn't quite as strict as the first one so is much easier for you to slip off occasionally and treat yourself and anyway it's another diet that eventually you'll abandon in the end albeit just a little at a time but you still end up eating the forbidden foods again and once more the weight creeps back on.

For nine out of ten people diets do not work. If they did there wouldn't be the obesity epidemic that is so prevalent in most of the western world. There are many different diets online and in the newspapers every week. Every so often a new 'super' diet is unveiled to the world that will change everyone who tries it into a sylph like creature within days. Walk round your local supermarket and see just how many overly obese men and women are wobbling up and down the aisle and then tell me that diets work.

If you still decide to try a diet then beware of the main diet wreaker, the treat day.

DO NOT HAVE A REGULAR TREAT DAY

Treat days are the killer of most diets. You cut the calories all week and are able to stick to your restricted diet because Sunday is your treat day. All the week is spent just waiting for Sunday to come round. After a hard week living on low calorie foods and small portions Sunday arrives at last but do you then have a treat? No, you pig out telling yourself that a chocolate bar and a glass or two of wine is just what you deserve after six days of abstinence. You then treat yourself to a much larger, and calorie laden, dinner than usual and an ice cream desert. So, all you have done is restrict the calories all week and then stuff them back in on your treat day.

A friend of mine has been on, what is considered to be one of the most popular weight loss diets for three years now so in theory he should be slim and maintaining his weight. Instead he loses a few pounds then puts them back on, then loses some more which soon go back on again and so on. This is because he insists he must have a treat day once a week when he eats like he hasn't seen food for years, almost certainly consuming many more calories on his treat day that he lost during the week. This not only nullifies the diet, but is probably not very good for his health. I am not saying never have a treat if you are on a diet just make sure it is not a regular treat day each week or so, when you spend the whole day giving yourself copious treats. If you have to treat yourself make sure that is what it is, a treat, not a multi-calorie laden banquet. The odd treat now and then will not do too much harm if you really must diet and at least it possibly keeps up the motivation to stick to the diet programme but I am convinced that diets do not work in the long term so why not try the BUSY method for losing the weight and keeping it off. Like my method for giving up smoking, it is not a quick fix but if it keeps off the pounds for the rest of your life then it has got to be worth the time and patience given to it. If you want to lose ten pounds before your holiday next month then this eating programme is possibly not for you, but if you want to lose your extra weight slowly and keep it off give it a try.

TRYING TO LOSE WEIGHT QUICKLY

So many people suddenly decide in July that they must lose weight before they go on their holiday in August, so they will look good laying on the beach. Or brides to be who think they must drop a dress size or two before the wedding in two or three months time. Many of them will succeed by embarking on very strict diets but, after the holiday or the wedding the diet is quickly forgotten and the weight they managed to lose goes back on in record time.

It is well known in the weight loss industry that the faster you lose weight the quicker it will go back on afterwards. It should also be remembered that going on something like a starvation diet might bring short term results but could also be very bad for your health indeed. Anyone who is significantly over weight should always talk to a doctor or nutritionist before embarking on any weight loss programme.

So we have established that some diets can be bad for your health. Lack of willpower makes many diets fail. Trying to lose weight too quickly makes diets fail. Giving yourself too many treat days makes diets fail. Ending a diet and going back to 'normal' eating usually ensures diets fail. Peer pressure "Go on one drink won't hurt". Often leads to a failed diet as well.

Is it any wonder that I say, don't go on a diet. So what can you do?

LOSE WEIGHT AND KEEP IT OFF FOREVER WITH THE BUSY METHOD

Firstly you must pick a date to start your weight loss programme at least two months ahead or preferably even three. This is to give you time to convince yourself that you can do it. As always, believe in yourself. Everyday in the run up to the programme and during, smile more and laugh more as in all BUSY programmes. As stated before, this will put you in a positive frame of mind convinced that you will succeed at this. Then choose three calorie laden foods that you can give up, forever, although don't let this statement frighten you, I will qualify it later. You must pick three food types that you think you can do without and that are quite fattening, it is not going to lose you much weight if you choose to give up onions, apples and blueberries. When I did the BUSY weight lose programme and lost 28 pounds, I chose potatoes, bread and alcohol. You are not going to give up your chosen foods until you reach your target weight, you are giving them up forever, more or less. I say more or less because if you go out for dinner with friends or to a party you are allowed to eat anything in moderation, assuming that you are not going out to dinner and parties several times each week. You look on these occasions as your little treats, when although eating anything offered, you do not over indulge. Not eating the three chosen foods at home will soon become a habit, a habit that is easy to follow and after a while you will find you do not miss those foods.

I also recommend you have two meat free days each week, fish once a week and chicken without the skin on, for two days. You will not generally feel hungry on this programme, because you can eat as many vegetables as you want and if you want to snack between meals eat fruit, but no more than twice per day.

As this is an eating programme it will need to suit both your appetite as well as your lifestyle because you will be on it forever. It can be altered every so often by reintroducing a food type you have given up and leaving out another of similar calorific content but always have three food types you have given up in your diet.

Here's some ideas of every day food items you can pick your three from, potatoes, rice, pasta, cakes, biscuits, bread, red meat, cheese, beans, chick peas, alcohol, sweets, chocolate, sugar, cream and deserts.

There is one other element to this programme and that is fasting. I disagree with fasting for a whole day or as some diets suggest, two days every week. This for most people is very difficult to sustain and could lead to you abandoning the programme altogether. What I suggest is that you choose a few hours during your day to go without any food and only drink water during this period. Fasting in moderation, is good for you, it gives your stomach a rest and speeds up your metabolism for when you next eat. I always fast from after dinner in the evening until around eleven o'clock the following morning, which is about fifteen or sixteen hours each day. Again if you happen to be out for dinner and it is served later in the evening, don't worry, it will only mean one or two hours less fasting and will do no harm to the programme. I realize the hours that I fast will not suit everybody so choose at least twelve hours, which suit you, when you eat nothing at all. Of course for the majority of these fasting hours you will probably be sleeping but make sure that your fasting period includes at least a third of the time when you are up and about.

This eating programme works for me, over six months I lost 12.9kgs, equal to 28.38 pounds. Because I lost it slowly there was little hardship and the weight stays off because I am continuing to eat roughly the same.

What part can exercise play in helping you to lose weight? We all need exercise but most of us, including me, can't get motivated to go to the gym or start jogging round the streets on a cold rainy morning for mile after mile. It is much easier however to exercise doing something that you find enjoyable. If you like dancing why not put some music on and dance around the room for half an hour or so. Do this two or three times a week and you will soon start to see the benefits. I have already stated in a previous chapter how laughing can help with weight loss and if you enjoy gardening that is another great way to get the exercise you need without the boredom of travelling to the gym and working up a sweat in front of strangers. In a United States study by the American Council on Exercise it was found that asking people to do just five minutes of housework per hour, such as washing up, folding laundry, ironing or cleaning resulted in an average 25% decrease in bad cholesterol across everybody who took part, and increased good cholesterol by an average of 21%. Exercise like this also slowly helped them to lose weight and researchers found that the overall benefits of just five minutes of household exercise per hour had the same benefits as an hour long gym workout. So there's no excuse for not getting that exercise we all need.

STOP SMOKING THE BUSY WAY

I have already described how I gave up smoking in Chapter 2 and how easy it was after trying many times before and finding it impossibly difficult. I smoked around two packs a day for twenty years, starting when I was just thirteen years of age, so could be described as a confirmed habitual smoking addict.

I didn't realize it at the time but after I discovered and refined the BUSY method I became aware that I had used part of the method to enable me to give up all those years before, without knowing what it was or how it worked.

To give up smoking use the same method to start the process as for the weight loss programme. Set a date as far ahead as you can, two or three months, or even more. Remember I planned six months ahead. During the run up to the date when you have decided to become a non-smoker, tell yourself every day that you will become a non-smoker from that date, visualize the benefits, your clothes and hair will not smell any more, smokers do stink you know. Your breath will be more pleasant, you will breath easier, have more energy and of course be saving a lot of money. As with all BUSY programmes start and end the day with a few minutes smiling and extra smiles, and laughter, throughout the day, whenever possible, as this will ensure a more positive frame of mind. Mentally count down the days to your stop smoking day and by the time you get to within a few days of the due date you will have convinced yourself that you are a non-smoker from that chosen day and you will be looking forward to ending that smoking habit. If a week or two before the chosen day you get the urge to give up there and then, resist it and force yourself to wait until the nominated day, as this will only strengthen your resolve and make the giving up even easier.

To help curb the physical side of the habit replace the act of having a cigarette dangling from your mouth, maybe use a fake cigarette or substitute of some kind. It might help to have plenty of sugar free chewing gum to hand, you can use this as much as you wish as gum is not addictive, so when you have broken the smoking habit after a few weeks, you will then be able to stop chewing gum if you wish.

As with all these things you must be positive and believe you can conquer the habit. I hear so many people say, " I can't give up smoking, I've tried so many times." What they have done is to convince themselves that they can't give up, they have told themselves so many times that they are unable to kick the habit that their brain accepts this fact and stops them giving up. It therefore follows that the opposite can happen. You can re-train your brain to accept that you can give up and it will do it for you. As with everything else in the BUSY method, believe and it will happen. One more piece of advice, from the day you give up do not tell friends and colleagues that you are trying to give up, tell them that you have given up, because that is the truth.

A lot of people say that Vaping helps to give up the smoking habit. As I have never tried it I cannot comment too much except to say that people that vape are still taking in nicotine, which is of course habit forming. Practising my BUSY method to give up smoking can get you the results you want without Vaping.

DEPRESSION AND ANXIETY

Depression and anxiety affect most people to a greater or lesser degree during their lives. For most people it passes eventually but there are people who suffer for much longer periods and find it almost takes over their life.

Serious cases of depression, sometimes called clinical depression, and anxiety should be treated with psychiatric and medical help from the professionals. That is not to say that it can't be cured using the BUSY method because in many cases it most certainly can and again I speak from personal experience.

I was in my late 20's living in a rented flat and working in the entertainment business. The summer had been spent at an east coast resort starring in a show for around three months. In the Autumn I was living at home and doing odd appearances in various venues when I developed a nervous stomach, sometimes known as 'butterflies in the stomach', for no apparent reason that I could deduce. This became more and more pronounced as the weeks passed and was there 24/7, my energy had gone and I was continually tired but was unable to sleep. Apart from that I was okay physically as far as I could tell. Then one day, a day that I shall never forget, I was sitting reading the newspaper when this dreadful feeling completely overwhelmed me and I knew that if I didn't do something immediately I would collapse. I ran out of the house and walked around the streets in the pouring rain in a state of blind panic but not knowing why this was happening to me. I had no immediate worries in my life, financial or personal and was at a loss to understand why this was happening and what in fact it was. My doctor agreed to see me later that day and diagnosed severe depression and anxiety and prescribed pills.

I cancelled some of my engagements and spent the days curled up on the couch wondering what the hell was happening to me. Up until this point I was a strong character, very laid back and certainly not the nervous kind, but now I was scared of my own shadow and was unable to make even the most simple decisions. Panic would set in every now and then and I seriously thought about ending my life rather than have this awful feeling of dread day and night, about which I could do nothing, even the copious amount of pills I was taking had no effect.

In the December I was committed to a contract in a theatre for six weeks, a contract I could not get out of so found somewhere to stay and started rehearsals for the production, all the time praying I would be able to get through it. Many times during this rehearsal period I felt the need to run out of the room but somehow managed to stay the course while popping ever more tranquilizers that still seemed to do nothing for me.

The show opened and the strange thing was that while on stage, smiling, laughing, and interacting with the audience, I felt fine and recall every performance standing in the finale line up thinking why can't this feeling last when I go off stage. The fact was though that as soon as I returned to my dressing room the awful feeling came over

111

me once more, like a black cloud descending until I was once again enveloped in this dark heavy doom laden fog.

Despite this happening every day I somehow managed to get through to the end of the contract and return home. Once again I retreated to the safety of my couch where I spent the days laying in the foetal position for perhaps three months, seeing nobody and doing nothing except to get more pills from my doctor who, I must say, never suggested any other help except to prescribe more pills. I remember thinking that I would not wish this feeling on my worst enemy, a feeling so intense that I would have done anything to make it go away. With hindsight it was probably a good thing that I wasn't functioning because if I had been I would possibly have taken an overdose just to get some peace.

Summer came and I had another contract to fulfill. It was a five month contract and I couldn't see how `I was going to get through it. I would have tried to pull out but by this time I needed the money badly. The first and most important thing was not to let any of my colleagues or the management know of my predicament and what a struggle it had become to get through each day. So from the beginning I pretended I was fine, laughing and joking with everyone and putting on a false front. Everyday telling myself I was fine and could do this. I had taken an apartment for the summer about a fifteen minute walk from the theatre I was appearing at and walked in every day.

After a few weeks of my daily walk and convincing myself I was fine and refusing to believe there was anything wrong with me but still living on the pills, I found that on some days as I walked in to work the dark cloud lifted for a while and I felt better. Ten minutes or so it would last at first, then after a while longer periods until by the end of the contract in late September I was feeling good for long periods, sometimes the whole day. I thought that perhaps something was helping me to get better and I became determined never to let the dark fog descend again.

When I got back home I stopped taking the pills and decided it was possibly the exercise, walking every day, that had helped me get through the depression so I continued to get as much exercise as I could convinced that I would soon be through this dark period in my life. By the next spring I was. I was feeling fine again and the depression, breakdown, whatever it was, has never affected me again.

What I know now is that the law of attraction was working to bring me out of the depression. Once I started convincing myself I was fine the law of attraction took over and eventually delivered the cure. Laughing and joking with my colleagues and of course appearing on stage every night and having to smile and laugh with the audience, although all false, put me in a more positive frame of mind and I have no doubt my daily walk helped, so once again what has become my BUSY method worked to deliver what I wanted and if you suffer from depression or anxiety follow the method and it will work for you as well.

FINANCE

Everybody needs help with their finances at sometime or other. Whether it is getting out of debt, where to invest savings, how to increase earnings, spending more wisely, or even what to do with all the money you've got. Ok so that last one probably doesn't apply to you, if it did I doubt you would be reading this book.

My BUSY method can show you how to manage your money more efficiently, how to manage your debts better, or even how to attract more money into your life, as much as you want.

Managing finance uses the same tools as managing anything else such as diet, health, smoking and so on. With the BUSY method you focus on the good, not the bad. To explain, if you spend your time focusing on the debt that you have, the money that you need, how to live on the money you earn, you will not only make yourself feel bad and probably think that the whole world is against you. You will also attract more of the same into your life, which is the very last thing you want to do.

By all means think constructively, decide which of your bills are the most important and therefore need to be given priority over others. Decide if there is anything in your life you can do without, magazine subscriptions, gym membership and the like, that will make your budget stretch further. Just getting down and depressed about your financial situation will do nothing to solve your problems, it will just make them seem much worse than they probably are and certainly won't bring any more money into your life.

Using the BUSY method will make you think more positively about money and put you in the right frame of mind to do something about it. There is a well known saying that states:

IT'S NOT WHAT YOU'VE GOT, IT'S WHAT YOU DO WITH IT THAT COUNTS.

This certainly applies to finances. You can be earning many thousands of pounds each month and still be in debt if you don't spend it wisely. So make a list of what you can do to make your money go further, to make sure you have money left at the end of the month rather than month left at the end of your money. There are plenty of web sites and newspaper columns with advice on how to do this. So change your utility suppliers and the company that holds your insurance for your car, house, contents, life policy and so on. We are told often that loyalty to these companies doesn't always pay and it is a good idea to shop around for better deals every year. I know this can be a chore sorting through all the comparison sites and I often hear people say that it is too much bother to change, when in fact in a couple of hours online you can change your car, building, contents, insurance, gas, electricity, telephone and broadband suppliers and even your bank accounts. All this can be arranged in a couple of hours once a year and will save you money. If you really can't be bothered to save money this way then you are either already very wealthy or not interested in becoming any wealthier.

With a positive outlook and focusing on being wealthy, having more than enough money to pay whatever bills come through your door, your brain will work towards ways of bringing more money into your life. Not just enough to cover the usual expenses in your day to day life but as much as you desire. Remember that the law of attraction states that like attracts like, so if you worry about money and the lack of it, it will attract more of the same, more worry and a bigger lack of money. If you start thinking that you already have all the money you need it will bring you more of the same.

Think like a wealthy person and you will become wealthy. A quick explanation though about what it is that constitutes wealth might be helpful at this point. Imagine a man who earns, say, £250,000 per year, a lot of money you may think, but supposing he has a house worth two million with a mortgage of one million, six children at school and heading towards university and all with expensive hobbies. Maybe a wife who needs a large car to carry the children on the school run and of course he needs a car to drive to the office every day. All of a sudden he doesn't seem very wealthy. Now imagine a man who earns just ten percent of what the other man earns, £25,000 per year, but he lives happily in a small two bedroom semi-detached house, left to him by his parents, so no mortgage to pay. He has no children, isn't keen on taking holidays and doesn't drive a car. He could be considered quite wealthy, so as I said at the start of this section on finance: It's not what you've got it's what you do with it, so visualize wealth rather that a monetary figure but however much money you want to become wealthy, once again believe it and you will receive it. It really is as simple as that with the law of attraction.

There are many ways you can save money if you give it some thought. I had a friend who paid for an expensive gym membership, he would drive the three miles from his home to the gym twice a week spend an hour or so on his work out then drive back home. He needed to cut his spending but insisted he needed the gym membership for the exercise and the health benefits it resulted in. I pointed out to him that if he ran to the gym instead of driving, didn't go in but turned round and ran back home that six mile run would almost give him the same health benefits as the gym work out did and he would save not only the cost of the membership but also the cost of the fuel for driving there and back.

Another useful little way to save money even if you don't have much spare, is to put just one penny in a pot on the first day of the year, on the second day you put two pennies in, on the third day three and so throughout the year. By the last day of the year you will put three hundred and sixty five pennies in and when you count it up you will find you have saved six hundred pounds without too much difficulty.

CHAPTER 13

WHAT PEOPLE THINK

ABOUT SMILING AND LAUGHTER

All the various components of my BUSY method have been known about for many hundreds of years and there have been many books published about self improvement and achieving success. My method has one ingredient that most books have either ignored or considered not part of an improvement programme but which I consider one of the most important for making my method work so well. It is also the one ingredient that is most likely to be ridiculed by some people as being of no apparent use in improving their lifestyle, career or health. The component I am talking about, and which I know is essential to self-improvement, is laughter and to a slightly lessor degree smiling.

If you read the chapter on laughter and smiling you will learn just how much research has gone into ascertaining the many benefits of these actions but the main benefits to the BUSY method are in releasing stress and creating a more positive attitude to enable the other components of the method to work at their most productive level.

If you smile and laugh on a daily basis you will be a happier and a healthier person. Over the years many prominent men and women have spoken on the benefits and importance of having laughter and the ability to smile as a major part of their life. Here follows a few quotes from some of them that might inspire you:

A day without laughter is a day wasted.

Charlie Chaplin 1898-1977. Actor and filmmaker.

We don't laugh because we're happy – we're happy because we laugh.
William James 1842-1910 Philosopher & Psychologist.

Laughter is great for you and it may even compare to a proper diet and exercise when it comes to keeping you healthy and disease free.
Dr. Lee Berk 1950 Associate professor at Loma Linda University, California.

At the height of laughter, the universe is flung into a kaleidoscope of new possibilities.
Jean Houston 1937 Co-founder of the Foundation for Mind Research.

You don't stop laughing because you grow old. You grow old because you stop laughing.
Michael Pritchard 1950 Comedian Youth counselor & Advocate of Social Emotional Learning.

A laugh is a smile that bursts.
Mary H Waltdrip 1914-1988 Author.

With the fearful strain that is on me night and day, if I did not laugh I should die.
Abraham Lincoln 1809-1865 16th President of the United States.

Let us always meet each other with a smile, for the smile is the beginning of love.
Mother Teresa 1910- 1997 Roman Catholic nun and missionary.

Smile, it is the key that fits the lock of everybody's heart.
Anthony J D'Angelo 1972 Writer and founder of Collegiate Empowerment.

Because of your smile you make life more beautiful.

Thich Nhat Hanh 1926   Vietnamese Buddhist Monk and peace activist.

ABOUT POSITIVITY

Most people know that it is better to be positive than negative and a person who is positive and optimistic about life in general will be happier, healthier, more able to deal with stress and generally more enthusiastic about life.

Positivity is not something you are born with just as negativity isn't. We can all teach ourselves to be more positive, it isn't difficult to replace a negative outlook with a positive one but it will take practise and as with most things, the more you practise the easier it will become and the better the results will be.

Being positive will show you how to succeed in everything you do, which is why it is an essential element of my BUSY method. If you approach the method while thinking that it will never work for you, you can be certain that it won't. Being positive is one of the secrets of a successful life.

Here's what other people have to say about positive thinking:

Be thankful for what you have; you'll end up having more. If you concentrate on what you don't have, you will never, ever have enough.
Oprah Winfrey 1954 Chat show host, Producer, Philanthropist.

In order to carry a positive action we must develop here a positive vision.
Dalai Lama 1935 Spiritual Leader Tibetan Buddhism.

I'm a very positive thinker, and I think that is what helps me the most in difficult moments.
Roger Federer 1981 Tennis Champion.

Once you replace negative thoughts with positive ones, you'll start having positive results.
Willie Nelson 1933 Singer Songwriter.

Positive thinking will let you do everything better than negative thinking will.
Zig Ziglar 1926-2012 Author and Motivational Speaker.

Pessimism leads to weakness, optimism to power.
William James 1842-1910 Philosopher and Psychologist.

The mind is everything, what you think you become.
Buddha Ascetic and Sage.

ABOUT VISUALIZATION

To visualize what you want, seeing it clearly and in great detail in your mind, is the start of the process of achieving whatever you want or want to be. First thing in the morning and last thing at night are good times to concentrate and 'see' whatever it is that you desire, but at any other time when you have a quiet few moments during your day, is also a good time to practise to visualize the object of your desires. It can be any number of things but you need to see each one clearly as if you already have or have achieved it.

As with all things practise makes perfect. You might find at the beginning that your mind wanders off the subject of your visualization when other thoughts push there way into your vision but don't let this put you off, after a while you will find that you are able to just concentrate on the one thing that you want. With practise you will eventually begin to believe that you already have what it is you are visualizing and once you believe, it will be delivered.

Many famous and successful people use visualization in their everyday lives and here is what some of them have to say about it:

Dreaming is not enough. You have to go a step further and use your imagination to visualize with intent! Forget everything you have ever been taught, and believe it will happen, just as you imagined it. That is the secret. That is the mystery of life.

Christine Anderson 1956 Actress.

If you can dream it, you can do it.
Walt Disney 1901-1966 Entrepreneur and Film producer.
It is true of the nation, as of the individual, that the greatest doer must also be a great dreamer.
Theodore Roosevelt 1858-1919 Statesmen author and President of the USA.

What the mind can conceive and believe it can achieve.
Napoleon Hill 1883-1970 Author of 'Think and Grow Rich'.

Visualize this thing that you want, see it, feel it, believe in it. Make your mental blue print and begin to build.
Robert Collier 1885-1950 Author.

To accomplish great things we must first dream, then visualize, then plan, believe, and act.
Alfred A Montapert 1906-1997 Author of 'The Supreme Philosophy of Man'.

The entrepreneur is essentially a visualizer. He can visualize something, and when he visualizes it he sees exactly how to make it happen.
Robert L Schwartz Lawyer and author.

Man can only receive what he sees himself receiving.
Florence Scovel Shinn 1971-1940 Metaphysical writer.

All prosperity begins in the mind and is dependent only upon the full use of our creative imagination.
Ruth Ross 1920-1982 Historian.

Dream lofty dreams, and as you dream, so shall you become. Your vision is the promise of what you shall at last unveil.

John Ruskin 1819-1900 Art critic Prominent social thinker Philanthropist.

Dare to visualize a world in which your most treasured dreams have become true.
Ralph Marston 1907-1967 American Football player.

ABOUT THE LAW OF ATTRACTION

The law of attraction is a very powerful law of the universe. It works for everyone even if you don't realize it is working. Some people assume and believe that nothing good ever happens to them, and guess what, nothing good ever does happen to them, because the law of attraction states, 'Like attracts like' so if you focus on bad things that happen in your life, more bad things will be attracted. This is not a new law or one that has just been discovered, it has been around for ever and is part of the law of the universe. Knowing how to use it is the secret of changing your life.

Many successful people admit to consciously using the law in both their personal and business life and attribute their success and happiness to the power of the law.

Here are just a few of the things people, past and present, have said about using the law.

Ask for what you want and be prepared to get it.
Maya Angelou 1928-2014 Civil Rights Activist Poet and Author

Whatever the mind can conceive it can achieve.
W. Clement Stone 1902-2002 Philanthropist and Author.

See yourself living in abundance and you will attract it.
Rhonda Byrne 1945 Writer and Producer.

What things soever ye desire, when ye pray, believe that ye receive them, and ye shall have them.
The Bible Mark 11:24

To accomplish great things we must not only act, but also dream; not only plan, but also believe.
Anatole France 1844-1924 Journalist and Novelist.

That which is like unto itself is drawn.
Esther Hicks 1948 Inspirational Speaker and Author

To bring anything into your life, imagine that it's already there.
Richard Bach 1936 Best selling Author.

You are the creator of your own reality.
Anonymous.

I attract to my life whatever I give my attention, energy and focus to, whether positive or negative.
Michael Losier 1962 Author of The Law of Attraction.

What you radiate outward in your thoughts, feelings, mental pictures and words, you attract into your life.
Catherine Ponder 1927 Minister of the Unity Church.

Imagination is everything, it is the preview of life's coming attractions.
Albert Einstein 1879-1955 Theoretical Psysicist

If you have read this far you will be ready to put the BUSY method into action. The method can be summed up in two words, focus and believe. Focus on what it is that you want, believe that you have it already and let your brain do the rest.

I said earlier that most humans only use a small percentage of their brain power so it doesn't take a genius to work out that we have a lot more power in the brain ready to be used at any time you decide, some say as much as 90% more. Just think if you had that much extra power ready for use in any thing else, your car, your central heating system, or all your domestic appliances, what a difference it would make to your life. So with that amount of dormant power ready for use in your brain imagine the changes you can make to your life.

The problem is that most people limit themselves all the time, telling themselves, "I couldn't do that." Or "I can't afford that." Or even "I'm not clever enough to achieve that." Well let me remind you that most all of us are born with the same faculties. You were born with exactly the same brain as Einstein and Shakespeare or any head of any bank or international company you like to name. It is a fact, that unless you were unfortunate enough to be born with brain damage you were born with the same brain as anyone else. The only difference between you and them is how you choose to use yours and how they choose to use theirs. My method will show you how and why you should unlock your brain and make more use of the enormous amount of unused power within.

We are nearly all guilty of limiting our use of the power contained in our brain by being far too negative and convincing ourselves we cannot do or achieve something when plainly we can. The most important part of my method is to get rid of the negativity and replace it with positivity. This will of course take practise, exactly how long it will take is not possible to say because it will depend on how negative you are when you start the process. Some people live a life of doom and gloom seeing just the bad side of everything while others see the good things in life with only a touch of negativity now and then. However once you have thrown out most of your negative outlook and replaced it with a more positive view you will certainly be a happier, a far less stressed person and will be ready to go on to the next step.

You will presumably have already written your lists of desires and gratitude so it is a small step to start visualizing those desires, and once you start visualizing your brain will use the law of attraction to bring into existence all the things you desire or in some cases, such as promotion, to get you up the next few steps of the career ladder and show you the way to achieve the success you want.

The most common excuse I hear from people who haven't managed to achieve whatever it is they thought they should have, is, " I haven't had the education I need, I am just not clever enough." Well there is no doubt that a good education will give you a head start in life, but remember it is never too late to learn, there are classes, both evening and daytime, available on almost any subject you can name. There are also many thousands of books available to read online, in libraries or that can be brought very cheaply from charity shops that can help you expand your knowledge on many subjects. Reading and thereby learning will not only enhance your understanding of whatever subject you decide on, it is also exercise for your brain.

We all know that if we don't exercise a muscle it will lose strength. If you went to bed and stayed there for a few weeks you would lose the ability to walk because the muscles would have weakened through lack of use. The brain is similar to a muscle, and therefore if you don't use it you will lose it. Your brain needs exercise just as much as your muscles, so keeping your brain active through regular use is essential. It doesn't matter what age you are or how much or how little education you have had, if you believe in yourself and exercise your brain you can still achieve anything you want if you have the determination. A good education might give you a head start but there are thousands of well educated people who don't seem to get on in life and many others who are much less educated but get to the top of their chosen ladders. There have been and still are many successful people throughout the ages and throughout the world who have achieved much in their business and personal lives who have had little or even no education.

Here are six people who despite not having the best education available still managed to become very successful by believing in themselves, being positive and being determined.

Richard Branson is founder of the Virgin group, which consists of over four hundred companies, and is estimated to be worth 5.1 billon dollars. That's not bad for a man who left school at the age of sixteen after, what his headmaster said was a poor academic performance, he stated that Branson would either end up in prison or become a millionaire. Richard Branson is also dyslexic and therefore finds reading and writing difficult. He didn't bother attending a university instead he started three businesses before he had even left school. The first, growing and selling Christmas trees, failed as did his second attempt, breeding and selling budgerigars. He refused to give up and his third attempt at starting a business, producing a magazine, named 'Student' at the age of just 16 became a success and within a year his net worth was estimated at £50,000. Four years later he started a mail order record business and opened a number of record stores that eventually became Virgin Megastores. He also opened a recording studio at his home in Oxford and rented studio time to many up and coming artistes. By 1981 he was involved in several businesses including package holidays. Among his many other business ventures at this time he also started an airline, Virgin Atlantic, a music label and most recently a space flight business, Virgin Galactic. In the year 2000, he was honoured with a knighthood from the Queen for services to entrepreneurship. He has stated that despite many set backs along the way it is his determination to succeed that has helped him reach his goals.

Henry Ford, born in 1863 was founder of the Ford Motor Company. He was born on a farm and left school at the age of thirteen and having had very little education. He was expected to work on his father's farm, which he did for the next three years. He then became an apprentice machinist at a ship building company. In his spare time he was experimenting with gasoline engines and at the age of twenty nine he built his first gasoline powered buggy. Nine years later he started the Ford motor Company. His first attempt at building cars failed after just two years because of the low quality and high cost. He battled on and seven years later, in 1908 invented the Model T Ford and by 1914 had sold over 250,000 of them. By 1918 half of all cars in America were Model T's. At his death in 1947 he was worth 188 billion dollars. With almost no education he had become one of the most successful business men in America.

Considered the greatest writer in the English language, William Shakespeare wrote around thirty nine plays and one hundred and fifty four sonnets during his comparatively short life. He was born around1564, and went to school until he was probably 12 or 13 years of age. As his family were not wealthy and all education had to be paid for it is certain that he wouldn't have had a particularly intensive education probably just learning to read, write and do basic maths. He started acting at the age of 18 and writing in his early twenties. He appears to have retired at the age of 49 so his writing career lasted a little over twenty years. It is estimated that four billion copies of his works have been sold to date. Although not a lot is known about his education except that he almost certainly left school in his early teens and didn't attend university. He was in effect not well schooled but despite this lack of education he is still considered the greatest British dramatist ever.

Steve Jobs was born in 1955 and has stated that he was not interested in his school years and learned very little. At 17 his adoptive parents enrolled him in college but he left after just six months to go travelling in India. Despite admitting that he had wasted his educational opportunities, at the age of 21 he became the co-founder of Apple Inc. and inventor, with Steve Wazniak, of the first successful personal computer. They went on to invent and market many other products including the IPod, IPhone and IPad. A millionaire many times over at his death in 2011 and despite only spending a few months at college and three years wandering around India and admitting that he enjoyed trying all kinds of drugs whilst there, became yet another incredibly successful man at a very early age without the benefit of any educational qualifications.

Guy Ritchie, a much respected film director of crime films, including, 'Lock Stock and Two Smoking Barrels', 'Revolver' and 'Sherlock Holmes'. The ex-husband of Madonna, he is considered one of the top five modern film directors with his movies making millions of dollars all over the world. He is though dyslexic and despite his privileged upbringing, had an unimpressive education. In fact he was thrown out of school at the age of fifteen, with no qualifications, for cutting classes too often and reportedly for drug use. He was also caught entertaining a girl in his room at the, all boys, boarding school, yet another reason for the schools decision to prematurely end his education. Undeterred he decided he wanted a career in the film industry but failed in his attempts to get into film school, instead talking his way into a job as a 'runner' on a film. His lack of education has not obviously hindered his climb to the top of his profession and his net worth today is estimated to be more than 150 million dollars.

Another man who has done well in his profession is Chris Dawson. He left school, after several years of learning very little, without any qualifications and being unable to read or write. Needless to say he couldn't find anyone who would give him a job so decided to become a market trader selling anything he could get his hands on. After building up his business he borrowed enough money to open his own discount shop in 1989 in the Devon town of Plymouth. Called 'The Range' he now owns 150 stores all over the country with a total value of around £2billion.
In 2017 this ex-market trader who couldn't read or write paid himself a dividend of £100million.

That is just six of the thousands of very successful people all over the world, who had little or no education but still managed to get to the top of their chosen professions despite, or maybe even because of, their personal problems and lack of a proper education. The fact is that none of them allowed their past to inhibit their future plans and ambitions. They all ploughed on regardless of all the obstructions they were to face and always made sure they learnt from their mistakes.

The exciting thing is that they were all born with exactly the same brain as you and I were. Their brains are wired no differently to yours and are no bigger or smaller, we are all born with the same brain. The difference is how you choose to use them and how determined you are to get the most out of your life.

Whether they knew it or not they all opened their mind, had a positive attitude and refused to let anything prevent them from reaching their goals. In other words they were determined, positive and believed in themselves.

There is nothing in the world that can stop you doing the same. By being as determined as they were and believing in yourself you can reach any goal you set yourself. So stop making excuses and start using my BUSY method to make your desires come to fruition. The only thing that can stop you doing this is you. The choice is yours.

Read it, believe it and make it work for you. Good luck.

[I would like to offer my grateful thanks to my good friend Rick Daniels who helped and encouraged me all the way in the writing of this book]

OTHER BOOKS BY THIS AUTHOR

THE PANTOMIME BOOK

Pantomime has been a popular type of entertainment in Britain since the Eighteenth century. Based on fairy tales and legends and performed by actors, singers and comedians, there are over two hundred productions performed in hundreds of theatres throughout the country every Christmas.

Many of the traditional gags and sketches used in all pantomime subjects since the Early Victorian period have been passed on through 'word of mouth' and have never been written down as a collection before.

The Pantomime Book is an hilarious selection of the most popular gags as well as being an invaluable source of comedy material for both professional and amateur actors, directors and producers. Together with theatrical anecdotes and helpful tips, it is also an interesting read for all pantomime enthusiasts.

BEYOND THE GLITTER

There are many different kinds of entertainment, from travelling fairs and circus to theatrical productions, radio, television, film and the music industry. Throughout history in all forms of the entertainment business you will find hard working, talented, honest participants. However there are also, and always have been, untalented, foolish, or dishonest people out to con the public and make a quick buck.

BEYOND THE GLITTER explores the mistakes, deceptions and fraudulent dealings in every type of entertainment throughout the years. Stories that are in turn hilarious or heartbreaking, dodgy or downright criminal. All are pure showbiz gossip that is, after all, just another part of the world of entertainment.

44578872R00078

Printed in Poland
by Amazon Fulfillment
Poland Sp. z o.o., Wrocław